Books sho...

CU00729530

2 2 MAR 1986   1 6 ...
                - 3 ...

    - 5 JUN 1986   3

1 4 AUG 1986   09. ... 94

1 9 SEP 1986   2 6 DEC 1988

                1 5 JAN 1990   1 9 OCT 1994

2 8 APR 1987   1 9 MAR 1990   1 5 NOV ...

- 5 AUG 1987   2 5 OCT 1990

                2 4 NOV 1990   1 4 DEC 1994

1 0 NOV 1987   28.JAN 2 4   6 FEB 1995

1 8 AUG 1988   1 3 JAN 1992   1 8 APR 1996

                1 7 NOV 1993

Other titles in Eagle Books

MY UNCLE HAD NOTHING TO DO WITH IT

Angus Macaulay

Illustrated by
Judith Allibone

Oxford University Press
Oxford   Toronto   Melbourne

Oxford University Press, Walton Street, Oxford OX2 6DP

Oxford   New York   Toronto
Delhi   Bombay   Calcutta   Madras   Karachi
Kuala Lumpur   Singapore   Hong Kong   Tokyo
Nairobi   Dar es Salaam   Cape Town
Melbourne   Auckland

and associated companies in
Beirut   Berlin   Ibadan   Mexico City   Nicosia

Oxford is a trade mark of Oxford Unviersity Press

© Angus Macaulay 1985

First published 1985

British Library Cataloguing in Publication Data

Macaulay, Angus
My uncle had nothing to do with it.
I. Title
823'.914[J]   PZ7

ISBN 0 19 271465 1

Typeset by Graphicraft Typesetters Ltd.
Printed in Hong Kong

Contents

1

The beginning (well, sort of . . .)

There was a lion, and he was called Boris, and he lived in a shed. The shed was on Uncle Joe's vegetable patch down towards the railway track. The vegetable patch really did belong to someone called 'Uncle Joe', because he was My Uncle and his name was Joe. The railway track belongs to someone else.

Uncle Joe was never *in* the shed when I saw him. He was always leaning on a different kind of spade and looking over at the railway. This was before I knew about Boris, of course. After a time, this began to bother me. Why wasn't Uncle Joe ever in his shed?

So, one day, I decided to TAKE STEPS.

'What's in the shed?' I asked him, as if I asked important questions like this every day.

'A lion,' he replied.

'What's its name?'

'Boris,' he said, quick as a flash.

I went over to the shed, leaned on the door, and tried to look through a hole in the wood.

'I shouldn't do that,' he said. 'They can be very ferocious, you know. Of course, he might be asleep,' he added. 'Boris likes to sleep a lot.'

I moved back from the door with a start. Perhaps I should be more careful.

Uncle Joe had turned his head away and was looking over at the railway again. I stepped up to the door again. This time I noticed that someone had piled a large heap of stones against the door. Just the sort of thing that someone who KNEW ABOUT LIONS would do to keep a sometimes ferocious lion inside. I put my head to the wood, but I couldn't hear any snoring. Perhaps Boris was awake, sitting in the darkness, breathing quietly to himself and wondering what to do.

I sniffed to see if there was any kind of PECULIAR SMELL. But all I could smell was the brown stuff that people put on their sheds. Lions don't smell like that, else they would say so on those films on TV. The ones where someone stands around in green shorts in the sun, looking at elephants through a telescope and telling you why they haven't got big ears.

I stepped away from the shed, and went back over to Uncle Joe.

'Promise you'll say hello to him when he wakes up?' I asked.

'I promise,' he said.

This was when I began to think of Uncle Joe as someone special. Usually he came to tea twice a week, leaned on his spade a lot, said nothing, smoked lots of pipes — and was about as interesting as a cold bath. Not like Uncle Mark, who was a BAD LOT and had to go to Burma (or was it Birmingham?) or Aunty Milly who kept cupboards full of soap, or the man in the green hat who told you he was going to Minsterly whenever you met him.

But after this, things picked up a lot, and when Uncle Joe next came to tea, he had two large parcels under his arms.

'Parcels,' I thought. 'Sealing wax! String! Exciting things in green cardboard!'

My Uncle stood on the doorstep wondering whether to come in. He always seemed surprised that our house was still where he left it last time. Very unfair. Just because bits of it exist on certain days of the week and not on others, especially the bits where things get lost. I suppose my family aren't entirely like everyone else's. Not everyone's Dad spends all day boiling up marmalade in big copper pots, and then spends all night building wooden sheds to put it in (just in case the corner shop runs out). And not everyone's Mum spends her time making model aeroplanes and hanging them in great FESTOONS round the house. But that's no reason to think that the house is unsafe to go in.

That's part of the trouble with Uncle Joe. All grown-up people do it — he DISAPPROVES. But here he was standing on the doorstep with two very interesting parcels, which I wanted to start opening. It didn't matter if they weren't for me.

'Come in, Uncle Joe,' I said and led him along the hall carefully. This isn't quite as silly as it sounds, because the cat had been swinging on the light-flex again, and had smashed the bulb. Besides which,

the floor was covered with roller-skates and balls of string. I didn't want him to drop the parcels.

At last, when he had hung his hat up and put his coat in a SAFE PLACE, we sat down on either side of the fire and looked at each other. I made a grab for the parcels. My Uncle cleared his throat suddenly, and I jumped. Then he scratched his nose and spoke. 'Muffins,' he said, looking closely at me.

I was a bit puzzled by this. Then I looked down at what was in the first parcel, as Uncle Joe had whisked the second one out of reach. Inside was a pile of pale buns with lots of holes in them. I looked underneath to see if there was any gunshot, but there wasn't.

'They're meant to be like that,' said My Uncle, reading my mind. 'They're Muffins. You eat them toasted. And you toast them with this.' (I thought they were crumpets because they were full of holes. But *he* said they were muffins. Oh, well.)

As he spoke, he produced the most unusual toasting-fork I had ever seen. When I asked him what it was, he didn't explain straight away, but started telling me a peculiar story, all about himself, and what he'd done between being like me and being all old and grumpy.

Most of it was pretty boring, except the bit at the end. This is the interesting bit, the way Uncle Joe told it:

'A long time ago,' he said, taking a deep breath,

'when I was younger and owned a fish-and-chip shop, I was told an important secret. All the fish and all the potatoes used by fish-and-chip shops come from a very special place at the end of the world, and arrive secretly by night on a chain of underground canals. This place at the end of the world is where THE BIGGEST HILL IN THE WORLD runs into the sea. On the hill they grow all the potatoes. And in the sea they catch all the fish. On the side of the hill live the tallest and thinnest possible potato-farmers. They have to be very tall and thin so that they don't roll down the hill if they fall over.'

'And the fishermen are the shortest and fattest possible,' I interrupted, 'so that they don't blow away in a strong wind.'

'Exactly! Of course, sometimes one of the farmers blows away, so they have to tie themselves down to their fences, if they're working in a strong wind, just to be safe. Even then, a sudden gust might take them, and in next to no time they're flying about like kites at the end of their tethers. And when they come down again, they have to sit down indoors wearing very heavy boots with concrete soles, just to get over the shock.'

'Do they like each other? The farmers and the fishermen, I mean.'

'They're the best of friends. Or rather, they were, until SOMETHING HAPPENED.'

'What happened?' I asked, wondering where all this was going.

'SOMEBODY who didn't want people to eat any more fish-and-chips started a quarrel between the two. Little things began to go wrong. Wheels disappeared off bicycles. The King of the Fishermen lost the whale that he was so fond of. The funnel of one of the fishing-boats was blocked with potato-peelings, so that it wouldn't start. This SOME-BODY sawed through the handles of the farmers' forks so that they snapped when they tried to dig things up. And after a while, each side began to suspect the other. The fishermen stopped rescuing farmers who blew away into the sea. And the farmers stopped pushing the fishermen's boats out to sea again when they ran aground.'

'Just a minute!' I said. 'This is all happening too quickly. How do they know it was a SOMEBODY who set them quarrelling, not one of them?'

'Because they're all too fond of fish-and-chips themselves to want to stop everyone else eating them.'

'Who is this SOMEBODY?'

'Nobody knows.'

'How long ago did all this happen?'

'The beginning of last week.'

'And what will happen if no one stops them?'

'Then', said My Uncle, eating the last muffin himself in the same way he'd eaten all the others, 'then the worst thing of all will happen. The AWFUL THING. They'll have a big showdown, and an even bigger punch-up, and since they're not very good at fighting, they'll all kill each other by mistake. And there will be no more fish-and-chips in the world. Think what that would mean.'

'There would be no fish-and-chips,' I said.

'What would we do on cold winter nights when there's nothing in the cupboard to eat?' said Uncle Joe.

'Saturday afternoon would not be the same without chips,' I said, biting my knuckle at this awful thought.

'The world will not go round as fast without chips,' said Uncle Joe.

'We must do something to stop them,' I interrupted him.

He looked at me.

Suddenly I could see that he was leading up to something. (I'm good at that. When Mr Hoddinot at school told me to go and see the Head, I knew that he was the one who'd seen me put lizards in all the teachers' pigeon-holes.)

Uncle Joe swept up the crumbs of all the muffins, crumbled them in a small bag, tipped them into another pipe (different from the one he was already smoking), and set fire to it all. Without using a match. Huge great coloured strings of smoke curled up to the ceiling like snakes. My Uncle spoke.

'Tom,' he said (that's my name, but it's not very important), 'will you come and help me stop the AWFUL THING from happening?'

How could I refuse? By saying no, I suppose. But I had another question.

'What is in the second parcel?'

My Uncle smiled. 'Always be careful with the second parcel. There isn't anything in the second parcel. I just brought it along to fool you. I would have put the toasting-fork in it, but it wouldn't fit. This is no ordinary toasting-fork, you know. I have been working on this for years and years in my shed and other people's sheds making it the most fearsome weapon known to modern science.'

'What about Boris?' I asked.

'Let's not think about Boris for the moment', he said. 'This fork can fly through the air, turn somersaults, and roast people three hundred yards away.' At this point the fork turned a quick back-flip to introduce itself.

'But the important thing,' he went on, 'is that you can use it to get from place to place faster. It can twist the strings that keep everywhere at the right distance from everywhere else, so that you don't have so far to go. Do you still want to come?'

'Yes,' I replied. 'But only to get out of doing the washing-up.'

He took it well. 'Right,' he said. 'To get to the end of the world, we have to do more than twist a few strings. We have to blow the bits in the middle, between here and the end of the world, I mean, just long enough for us to get through to the other side.'

And as he spoke, he beat on the fireplace with the fork. In through seven doors came my seven cousins. I haven't mentioned them before, because I'm never sure if there really are seven of them. They all look alike, and they never usually appear in the same place at the same time. Anyway, here they were, carrying an enormous balloon and seven different kinds of pump. My Uncle arranged the balloons on the hearth rug (which was a dog half the time) and took a small pin out of his pocket.

'Pump it up,' he said. The balloon swelled up till it was bigger than my head . . . bigger than me . . . bigger than the sofa . . . and finally it blocked out the windows.

Unlike real balloons that carry people, this one didn't have a basket underneath. Instead, there were a few rope handles to hold on to. Uncle Joe grabbed one and I grabbed a lot, in case it was safer that way. Uncle Joe then stuck the pin into the balloon. It didn't go off with a BANG, but blew air out at amazing speed. The balloon shot off at such a speed that it went through walls and buildings and all sorts of other things without having to go round them. This was all too much for me and I closed my eyes.

After a long time when I kept my eyes tight shut,

we touched down on something wet and started to sink. Very gracefully, but sinking all the same.

And all these fish clustered round us, making

rude remarks about the road sign which Uncle Joe seemed to have grabbed up on the way.

'What are we going to do?' I asked. My Uncle didn't reply. He was looking surprised again. I quickly tied a knot in as many bits of the balloon as I could, to keep us afloat. By then the fish were making very rude remarks about me as well, so I gave them some remarks back about *hooks* and *nets*, which seemed to scare the biggest of them, an evil fat thing with big red lips and fog-lamps for eyes. He turned and dived out of sight, taking the rest of the fishes with him, and we both breathed a sigh of relief, or some sort of sigh.

I took a good look above me and below me. Several times. Then at my reflection in the water. Lastly I took a look at THE BIGGEST HILL IN THE WORLD. Not only was it very big, it was also very fat and had three arms that stuck out into the sea. The whole thing looked like an octopus with a few bits missing. It wasn't moving (not much anyway) so it couldn't be an octopus. Could it?

I decided not to turn my back on it in case it tried to eat me. What a way for the world to end, though. Just this hill and all this sea, which I suppose must be the biggest sea in the world. It was certainly a good size for a sea. And it looked like it went everywhere.

My Uncle came to life at last.

'Action,' he said. 'As we've landed here, we may

as well go and see the King of the Fishermen and ask him what's going on. If he won't help, we'll go to the Chief of the Farmers. The only thing to do is see everybody as fast as possible and stop them from the AWFUL THING. Just blow into this bag, please.'

He offered me a large green balloon (GREEN FOR GO, I thought), which I blew up to blow us along, while he paddled frantically with the road sign. NO WAITING, it said.

That certainly seemed to be the way things were happening today. The small balloon lost its puff, and I had to blow it up again. As I let it go, I noticed that we were being followed by the fish with the big red lips. It was a lot angrier than before and kept flashing its teeth at us. Unless all that flashing was really meant to be a signal. It was catching us up! I could hear it breathing! I could smell yesterday's dinner on its breath (mostly onions)!

Just as it caught up with us, My Uncle dealt it a hefty whack on the side of the head with the road sign. It rolled over on its back like a dog, but I didn't think somehow that it wanted to be scratched.

'UUUUUUuuuuuu,' it gasped. 'It was ... the one who did it was ... it was ...'

Before it could finish its sentence, it sank. We both of us knew that we had done *a wrong thing*. But before we could even start to do something about it, the balloon started to sink again. My Uncle must have punctured it when he clobbered the fish.

'This is it,' I thought. 'I should have stayed and done the washing-up after all.'

'Swim for it!' yelled My Uncle and jumped into the sea.

'HEEEEEELPPP,' I shouted, before jumping, just in case there was anyone chugging about in a lifeboat with nothing better to do. The water was a lot worse than the cold tap, and there was a lot of seaweed snaking at my legs. It was green and very wavy, and there were little squiggles darting in and out of the strands.

I kicked at it and freed one leg, only to get the other leg even more caught up. I tried with my left arm, but that got stuck as well. Then I realized that it was My Uncle's leg that my hand was caught up with. That improved things a bit. At least I could wriggle about and try to attract attention to myself. (Don't I usually?)

'Help,' I shouted. 'Why can't anyone hear me? Why did I come? Am I going to get any wetter? Is there an end to all this?'

2

The King of the Fishermen,
and other people

The end to all this was a short fat man called Sam in
a small red rowing-boat. I knew he was called Sam
because it was written in broad yellow letters on his

oilskin. Neither of us noticed him till we bumped
our heads against one of his oars.

'Sorry,' we both said.

'Oh! Oh, sorry,' he replied, peering down at us.
'Have you seen my glasses anywhere? I can't row
straight without them.'

Heaving ourselves on board over the end of the
boat to stop it tipping over, we poked around in the

water and dead leaves at the bottom of the boat. No glasses anywhere to be seen.

'That was a near thing,' said Uncle Joe. 'If you hadn't come by then, we might both have drowned.'

'Ah,' said Sam, 'that's very kind of you, but I don't really know what I'm doing. I haven't for days. You can't see my memory anywhere, can you? I've lost that as well, I think. I suppose that we won't be able to say who we are, because I won't remember yours, and I can't remember what mine is to be sure. Names, I mean. Perhaps you'd better take the oars. At least when we've arrived somewhere, they might be able to tell us where we should be going.'

'Wait,' I interrupted him. 'Did you say that you were supposed to be going somewhere to do something? Are you going to fight a battle?'

'Battle,' said Sam. 'Well I'm not really sure. I know that something didn't quite feel right when I woke up this morning, whatever or whenever this morning was,' he added, staring off into the distance.

'He doesn't look very good, does he?' whispered My Uncle.

'We've got to act a bit quicker than I thought. Here, take this oar. We'll head over there. It sounds noisy enough to be something important.'

Slowly, slowly from afar (**POETRY**) came the sound of music. Well, sort of music. There was rather more rattling and whistling in it than the stuff you get on the radio, but it still made me want to misbehave, so it must have been all right.

As we approached, I saw a large sign: KING'S PALACE — TURN LEFT OR RIGHT, it said.

Since the palace or hut or shed was just behind the sign, I suppose it was quite sensible. But if all the signs leading the way there had been like that, I thought — well at least we wouldn't have had to ask the way. Because everybody else would be just as lost as us.

A wave in the face put a stop to all this DEEP THORT. It also made me take a look at the palace properly. For a start, it looked more like a floating shed than a palace, though it was tidier than most sheds.

There was also a large area all round the shed covered in blue bouncy mattresses. And all over this, another short fat man in bright orange oilskins was dancing and waving a rattle. He had to be the King because it was written all over him in black

letters. Also he was taller and thinner than the others, even though he was still a short fat man. Behind him, blowing whistles of various shapes, were other short fat men, with their names written on their backs like Sam's was.

I was just getting interested in these goings-on, when Uncle Joe took out another pipe.

'This is just so that people can't see us coming,' he said, puffing huge great thick greasy clouds of smoke in the direction of the shed. I didn't tell him that someone might wonder where all that smoke was coming from. After all, it didn't look much like rain-clouds.

'What if we can't see where we're going?' I was about to ask, when I noticed that Uncle Joe was wearing an unusually thick pair of glasses. A thing he never did, since he can see as well (or as badly) as everyone else.

'Disguise,' he hissed at me, when I pointed at them. I was about to give him a CRISP REPLY when the rowing-boat cannoned into the side of the shed. Uncle Joe leaped out to tie the boat up, but fell over his own feet, because he couldn't see where they were.

'Take those glasses off, Uncle Joe,' I said, coming to his rescue, 'and give them back to the man who can't remember his name. They may not be his glasses but he needs a pair, and you don't.'

Uncle Joe agreed, gave them back, and started puffing a lot harder on his pipe.

'O oooo,' said the short man in the rowing-boat. 'I can't tell you how much better that is. Everything's small and smudged again. I can't be doing with things that look all clear and bright.'

This was too much for me to cope with all at once, so I tied the boat up with my tightest knot, and felt my way through the smoke onto the mattresses surrounding the shed. There was still a lot of rattling and whistling, but it all came from inside.

'Does everybody here see things like you?' I asked the short man.

'Everyone except the King,' he said. 'And he sees everything blurred without the help of glasses. That's why he's King.'

'Has it always been like this?'

'I think so, but I can't remember. I don't suppose your friend has borrowed it as another bit of disguise? My memory, I mean. I think that's the thing I've lost.'

'I hope not,' I said, and coughed fiercely for several minutes because of the smoke. When I looked up, the man had gone. Perhaps my knot wasn't that special after all. Or perhaps he'd managed to lose himself *and* his rowing-boat, just to make things worse for him.

I ducked through a gap in the smoke, and found a doorway. Unfortunately it wasn't attached to anything useful, like a room, so I looked round again. This time I got the right one, leading into a sort of cabin, a lot larger inside than it was outside. But I didn't let this bother me, as the King probably hadn't noticed.

The inside of the cabin was festooned with all kinds of practical things, such as lobster-pots and oilskins in various colours, and lots of unlikely objects for a fisherman: bicycle pumps, and biscuit tins full of milk-bottle tops, coat-hangers strung

26

together with red string, and bundles of pokers.
Perhaps the King found it difficult to throw things
away.

And there he was, the King of the Fishermen,
sitting in a big red rocking-chair playing chess
with a dark thin twisted man, who looked like
a snake trying to stand at attention. The dark thin
man was sitting right in the corner, sipping all the
time at a thin twisted cup with cobwebs all over the
handle. He didn't let me get any further into the
room, but stood up, still keeping his face in shadow,
and brought his teeth together with a resounding
SNAPPP. The King and all his whistle-blowers
jumped.

'And what is this?' snarled the dark thin man.
'Some evil creature that has been hiding at the
bottom of the sea, I shouldn't wonder. I trust Your

Majesty will take notice of the fact that it is not blurred. I think we should kill it straight away, because

1) it's not good to eat,
2) I don't like strangers,
3) I can see it clearly,
4) I can only think of three reasons to get rid of it. Does anybody dare disagree?'

As he spoke these last few words he gave a most menacing snap of a lot of fingers (all his own), shook himself with a dry clatter, and sat down again.

The King didn't seem to have noticed this unfriendly welcome, and carried on staring at the chess board. Then he turned, rattled his rattle, and looked over at me.

'Nonononono,' he said rather quickly, 'No, Plover, it can't be a *creature* because it looks ... sort of ... egg-shaped' (at this point he swept the front of his head with his hand) ... 'anyway, whatever it is, I must say hullo to it. We'll have to finish this game tomorrow. This game has been going on for longer than I can remember, so a little longer ...'

(here he stopped, swept the front of his head again, and tried to start talking about something else) ... 'and besides, there are two of them.'

At this precise moment, Uncle Joe came in. Well, fell in. The smoke was a bit thick round the door. So much for not being noticed when we arrived.

The King waved cheerfully at him.

'I would welcome both of you,' he said, 'but I've just got to go off and win a battle.'

'AAaaa,' said Uncle Joe, as if he knew just what to do.

'Don't listen to him,' said the dark twisted Plover, moving into the light and flashing his pointed teeth at everyone. 'They're the sort of people who think that we shouldn't pay back the farmers for the DREADFUL THING that they did. And what did they do?'

'They stole our whale and that means WAR,' shouted the whistle-blowers, and gave a huge blast on their whistles.

For once, Plover seemed pleased. But the King wasn't so sure. He took a long time to speak, though, and had to scratch his head and tug his ears for a long time first.

'Well,' he said, 'I felt it was something I *ought* to do. I don't really think I like fighting but perhaps it's good for me to do this sort of thing from time to time. I do hope you're not angry about it. Perhaps we should wait. Till this evening. That is, if you two don't really think we should go off and fight?'

'No, we don't,' I said quickly, before Plover could open his mouth. 'As I thought,' said the King dreamily. 'You really are shaped very much like eggs, both of you. I haven't seen such egg-shaped people for ... however long it was.... Have you read my book about the whale? It's called *101 Things you need to Know if you Want to Keep a Whale at Home.*'

'But people don't keep whales at home,' I said. 'They go out in large boats with harpoons and knives, to kill them and cut them up and make them into oil.'

There was a horrible silence. The King tried to look at me over the top of his glasses, then remembered that he wasn't wearing any.

'Do you mean to say that somewhere over there, people don't look after their whales properly? You're not just saying that to shock me because I've never seen you before?'

'TREASON!' hissed Plover.

'Yes,' I said, because it was true.

'Well, well,' said the King. 'Perhaps it was someone from ... you know ... over-there-where-they-treat-whales-badly ... who took her away. Do you know I used to sing to her? I had a whole bookful of songs that she was fond of....' He sighed.

'There is one thing we could do,' said Uncle Joe, lighting his pipe. 'We could go and find out what's happened to your whale. And even if the Farmers-

30

who-live-up-on-the-hill have done something with her, I'm sure that we could get the Chief of the Farmers to come and say he's sorry, or explain why or even play chess. . . .'

'What a brilliant idea,' said the King, leaning back in his throne. 'Fix it all up someone, will you? I must just do nothing for a while.'

With that he spun the throne round and began to do nothing very quietly facing the opposite wall.

Through a thin cloud of smoke I could see My Uncle smile, probably at me, since he didn't know anyone else there. Perhaps he ought to have known somebody? After all who would set off for the other end of the world to do acts of daring, without having a vague idea of who and what to expect? But then, grown-up people have always been a slight mystery to me. I'm hoping I can get to that age without these odd things that they have to go through. They're never the same again.

One of the whistle-blowing fishermen shuffled over to me. 'You can borrow my boat,' he breathed through a mouthful of broken teeth. 'It's the one on the left.'

He shuffled off, leaving me with a slight smell of kippers and no idea of what he meant. I made signals to Uncle Joe, and he put out his pipe and followed me out of the door. There were thirty boats on the left, all looking exactly the same. So we picked the nearest one and got in.

'Where should we go?' I asked.

'Head for the middle one of those arms,' said Uncle Joe. 'I like the shape.'

'Arms of what?' I said.

'Arms of the hill,' he said, and showed me on the map. Well, it did have three lumpy bits that stuck out a bit like arms, I suppose.

By the time we'd reached the middle one, I could see what he meant. 'Now,' he said, unfolding another large map, 'there should be a way in somewhere down on the left.'

'Way into what?' I asked.

'Way into the hill,' replied Uncle Joe crisply, fingering his toasting-fork. 'Potatoes grow with the interesting bits underground. Therefore the Chief Farmer, to make things simpler, lives underground too. A lot of the other farmers have started to do the same. It means that they don't get blown away so often, and they don't have to go out and dig up all their potatoes from above: they build tunnels underground and pick the potatoes from below.'

'What a strange place,' I said.

'It's a lot more sensible than you think,' said Uncle Joe, pushing the boat the last few yards up on to the beach with the toasting-fork, and tying the rope to a rock.

Three paces to the left I could see a large inviting doorway, wide enough to hold at least five tall thin men, probably with five tall thin dogs as well.

'Hold this,' said Uncle Joe, giving me the toasting-fork. 'You need both hands to knock on a door like this.' He beat loudly on the door several times and kicked it twice, just to be on the safe side.

Just then I heard a flutter of wings. Above us, a great flock of gulls was rocketing away from something it didn't like the look of. And that something was dark and thin and twisted. And it was coming across the beach towards us. I tried to get the fork to do something, but it wouldn't. Perhaps I didn't say 'Please'. By the time my mouth had decided to open and ask Uncle Joe what to do, we had been seized, expertly tied up, and thrust through a thin doorway on the right of the first one.

'I don't like spies,' said Plover, grinding his teeth and crackling his knuckles, then cracking his teeth and grinding his knuckles (the second one was more painful, and he had to stop).

'Spy!' said I. 'Spy yourself,' then wished I hadn't.

Plover smiled. 'Do you know where this tunnel leads?' he asked. 'I shall tell you. It leads to the onion-pickling room. As a punishment for getting in my way, I am going to have you well and truly pickled. And I'm going to blame it on the farmers, so that everyone carries on fighting. I've got plans, you know. I want to get rid of everyone here and knock this horrible hill over. When I've done that, the world's supply of fish-and-chips will disappear, and I will be able to make them give me anything I want to bring fish-and-chips back. I shall be the most powerful man in the world.' As he said this, he laughed and crackled his knuckles.

3

Evil things underground

Heroes don't usually tell you about the bits in the story when they don't know what to do. Unfortunately I can't tell you about anything else, since in this story there are no beautiful maidens with raven-black hair and skin like marble being led away, kicking and struggling, by the servants of the evil Count — unless I cheat, of course.

Supposing I was to tell you about my friend Terri who can see ghosts? She says it's because she's got a third eye in the back of her head. I don't believe her because I've looked for ages and all I ever found was this bald place where she cut her head falling off the bus. Even if she is lying, it's nice to know that there are at least seven shapes hovering unseen over the biscuit tin in the kitchen. Not including me.

Actually, she was right about the SHAPE. The Shape is this very tall thing shaped like a boiler which stands in the way and stops you getting into the bathroom. It also hangs things on the back of the door, but only green things like the towel. There may not be any ghosts, but there is a SHAPE because I've seen it through the spotty glass at the top of the door.

As soon as Terri walked in, she knew. 'There's a

shape in this house,' she said. 'Something mischievous. But I've told it to go away. It's heard me. It's looking at me. It's going out through the cat-door. It's climbing up the wall — now it's over the house and flying away. I don't think it's going to come back. It won't do anything if it does.'

And it didn't. Even if she can get rid of things like the shape, I'm not really sure if she is my friend. After all she is forty-nine days older than me, which is pretty unforgivable. But then she can't eat pineapple chunks, because they bring her out in funny spots, so I usually get hers. Decisions, decisions. It's so hard being me sometimes. . . .

It didn't fool you, did it? You can still remember that I'm tied up and stuck in a wheelbarrow and

heading for a horrible pickly end, unable to help

36

myself or my Uncle Joe. I didn't tell you about the wheelbarrow, did I? If you'd seen it, you wouldn't have mentioned it either. Nor would Uncle Joe, because he had a sack over his head.

At times like this, my friend Terri, who has a lot to say on every occasion (more than me anyway, which takes some doing), would say this: *if you can't think of something sensible, think of something really silly.* So I did, as I tried to work out how long it was before we reached the end of the road. I thought of the fattest man in the blackest coat with the yellowest gum-boots imaginable, a four-wheeled python, a beard so large it would have to be kept indoors. These didn't help a lot, but they kept me from thinking about HOT VINEGAR and old onion skins.

I thought again: a man the size of a saxophone, a saxophone the size of a man, a piece of wood seventeen seconds long, a skating cat who lived in a graveyard....

These wonderful thoughts were brought to a quick end as the wheelbarrow rounded a corner into a big cave, and the strong smell that had been oozing along the tunnel came right up to us and socked us in the nose. Plover tipped up the wheelbarrow and we collapsed in a heap.

I looked up and saw a huge machine with belts and pulleys everywhere. One belt had buckets attached to it all the way up. Plover switched the machine on, and I watched as the buckets went up to the top, tipped what was in them on to another belt, and came down empty. The belt at the top was

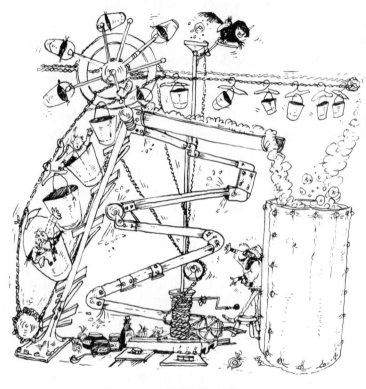

flat and moved everything along to a far corner of the cave, where a huge vat bubbled and sent out thick steam and smoke. Everything about the machine was huge. It must have been at least as tall as a house and as long as a football pitch.

'Pickling time!' sneered Plover. 'This will teach you not to get in my way. Nobody is too tough a nut for me to crack.' And as he said the word 'crack', he snapped all his knuckles at once. Ugh. When he saw that I didn't like it, he took hold of his neck and clicked it a few times. Ugh, ugh.

Then he pointed at the huge vat in the corner that was bubbling and filling the room with the SMELL. At that moment, I wished that I could have got rid of it as easily as Terri got rid of the SHAPE.

'That smell', gurgled Plover, 'is hot vinegar. Not only will you both die horribly, you will also smell REVOLTINGLY nasty. Even if you do manage to escape, which of course is impossible, my dogs will be able to sniff you from miles away.' And with a gurgling sort of laugh, he tied us inside a large bucket.

'Goodbye,' he said, and blew us a kiss. Ugh, ugh, ugh.

'What are we going to do?' I asked Uncle Joe as we heard Plover walking away. I turned round to look at him, and a familiar smell hit me. Yes, he was smoking another pipe. And better still, he didn't seem to be tied up any more.

'Don't move,' he said through a mouthful of teeth, producing from behind his back the toasting-fork. . . . I gaped, as he cut the ropes tying me with one swift blow from the fork, and stopped the machine with a quick bolt of lightning from the left-hand prong of the toasting fork.

'Go get him,' whispered Uncle Joe to the fork, and it took off up the tunnel like a well-squeezed piece of soap. There was a loud howl, and the sound of a door slamming.

'He won't be able to sit down for quite a while,' said Uncle Joe. 'That means he won't cause any trouble for quite a while either. He looks the sort of person who only causes trouble sitting down.'

I nodded because I couldn't really see what he was talking about, and because I was wondering how we were going to get down.

'We need a ladder,' I said.

'Can't we use the toasting-fork?' said Uncle Joe, trying to light his (empty) pipe.

'You can't climb down a toasting-fork,' I said. 'Not very far anyway. They taught me that at school. Besides, don't be stupid, the fork is still halfway up the tunnel.'

Uncle Joe saw that this was true, and whistled in a strange way to make the fork come back to him.

I thought for a bit. We still didn't have a ladder. But we still had the ropes that Plover had tied us up with. With a knot or two they should reach somewhere a bit nearer the ground, I thought.

As I was thinking this thought, the toasting-fork returned to Uncle Joe in a sudden sort of way. We both jumped.

'Can you make the machine turn backwards?' I

asked, when we had both stopped being surprised.

'No,' said Uncle Joe, 'because I don't know what lever to work. We'll have to tie the rope together and climb down it. It's our only way out.'

I didn't like the idea of this, but what can you do in DANGEROUS MOMENTS with Uncles? You have to let them have their way.

I tied and tied and tied and tied. And then I tied again, and again a bit later. At last the rope was all knotted together. I held the end tight and let it down over the side of the bucket we were standing in. It reached the floor, which was good, but the floor seemed a long way away.

Five thousand feet at least. Well, not quite five thousand. Perhaps three

and a half thousand. A long way, anyhow, even if it wasn't five, or three and a half thousand.

I tied the rope to the top of the bucket with a special knot, and we both started to climb down. I didn't like it much because I remembered the time I came down a rope too fast in the gym and had sore hands for a week. I climbed down slowly and Uncle Joe climbed down slowly and we hated every minute of it. I won't tell you any more.

Anyway I got down at last, and so did Uncle Joe, which is why there's still a story and not a great line of stars like this ******************************

Or a long silence, like you get in films when they don't want to show you the interesting bits.

They're not always quite this shape (the silences), but you know the sort of thing. . . . Mind you don't cut yourselves on the sharp ends.

When we'd touched down, we then had to decide where? and why? and with who? and what to do anyway? and does it really matter?

We decided in the end that it did matter, and that we should go next door and tell the Chief of the Farmers a few useful things. Such as: what he ought to do with Plover when he next saw him.

As there was a lot of darkness in the cave, and not a lot of light, we had to feel our way along the wall to find the entrance to the tunnel and the way out and fresh air and all that sort of rubbish. . . .

I shuddered and quivered all the way. The wall was as clammy as a lizard's bathroom, not to mention the lizards (I won't, I promise). I can't tell you much more about the tunnel. I mean, I might just as well tell you about the dark side of the moon, or something else I can't see. If you want to know what it was like, it was like the BAD THING AT STOKE GABRIEL, which made the cat's hair turn white. Enough said.

When we'd come out of one long dark slimy tunnel, we were on the beach again. Instead of using our heads and running away, we went along to where the Chief Farmer's Cave was, and knocked on the door. There was no reply.

We beat on the large door again, and a thin man leapt out at us. 'Visitors to see the Chief of the Farmers?' he asked and whisked us into a room at the side before we had a chance to say yes or no. When I say whisked, I really do mean whisked, because he carried a large feather duster, which he used to keep everything at arm's length.

We tried to sit down, but there was nothing to sit on. The thin man smiled, as if this was his favourite joke.

He didn't have much time to enjoy this one, because there was a huge crash and a cloud of dust as a messenger arrived on roller-skates, forgetting to

stop at the end of the passage as he did so. The whole passage, from ceiling to floor, was made of red brick, and it looked as if the messenger did this every day. Perhaps they had to find a new messenger every day and the old one could never tell the new one because he had knocked all his teeth out on the end of the passage?

This time, he'd only managed to lose a wheel off his roller-skates, so all was not so bad. But he was so out of breath that he could only point at us, then

point up the passage with his thumb.

We started to walk up this passage. It was a very

44

long passage, and full of strange lumps that got caught in between the toes. At last, it widened and grew all sorts of small arches and store-holes that all had to be dusted before we could pass them by.

We took a sweeping left and wound up in what must have been the throne-room, because there was nothing but a throne in it, and another thin man

sitting on it. He was rather shorter and fatter than the man at the door with the duster. (So would you be if you sat about indoors all day not getting blown about by evil-minded winds, or digging up potatoes. But I still think it's better to be a fat man than a thin man. All my favourite people are really fat, like wrestlers and cooks. I'm sure they're happier like that. I'm going to be really fat if they let me.)

All this DEEP THORT was interrupted by the thinfat man on the throne suddenly noticing us, and greeting us with a wave and a bow. We waved back and bowed as well as we could after all the bumping and bruising that kept happening. The next adventure I go on, I shall ask about this before I go.

But who would I ask? Is there a special place with cards up in the window like: 'WANTED, someone for adventure. Must not ask too many questions.' And I would go in, and ask how many questions is too many, and they would say, 'One question is too many, please go away, we don't want you. . . .'

After wrestling with his mouth for several seconds, the thinfat man opened it. 'We've run out of straws to chew,' he said, 'and I can't get used to chewing-gum. What can I do for you? Have you come to cause trouble, to look for treasure, to steal my potatoes, or just to have a swim?'

This was a tricky one, and we didn't answer for six or several moments.

'Well,' he said, 'you might answer. Don't you know there's a war on?'

'Why?' I asked, and wished I hadn't. This is the sort of thing that people get clapped in irons for.

'Because', said the thinfat man, 'we are going to win. That's the first reason. Secondly, the fishermen cannot be allowed to get away with whatever it was that they got away with. I can't remember what it was, in fact I don't think that I ever knew. But it was something so amazingly evil that nobody could ever know what it was. I couldn't even find it in my copy of *5,999 Evil Things That Kings and Chiefs should Beware of.* Perhaps I should write it down in the blank pages at the end. And thirdly, my chief spy Plover tells me it's the right thing to do.'

'But Plover also works for the King of the Fishermen', interrupted Uncle Joe.

'He's not just a spy,' said the Chief Farmer sharply, 'he's a DOUBLE AGENT, like they have in all those boring films on television. He works for both sides, so he does the work of two people. But he's only one person, so I only have to pay him enough for one. Very handy. Saves me money.'

'Anyway, who are you?' he went on. 'You're not the right shape to be from these parts. I don't think I trust either of you. I'm sure you're all right really, but I shall just have to have you put to death. One never knows, does one?' With that he blew a large whistle, and a huge dog came in. The huge dog produced an even larger whistle, blew it and in walked Plover. He blew on an enormous whistle, whereupon (GRAMMAR) three very evil-looking cronies of his shuffled, sidled, and crawled in.

'These are the intruders, Your Chiefness,' said Plover oozily. 'Shall I deal with them? We have to wait till this evening before we can fight, which should be another three hours by my watch. These no-good meddlers have already stopped the King of the Fishermen from going out to fight immediately.'

I don't know what surprised me more, seeing Plover back and double-crossing everyone, or the

Chief of the Farmers being so unpleased to see two friendly strangers about to do an AMAZINGLY GOOD DEED, i.e. stopping the fishermen and farmers killing each other and cutting off the entire supply of fish-and-chips to the world, and in fact causing the world to end rather a long time before the end of the second half. Not forgetting injury time, which Uncle Joe and I certainly needed to get over all the bumps, etc., and possibly to generally duff up and work over Plover for being such a mean rotten twister.

'Let me introduce you to my assistants,' snarled

Plover, dropping back into his usual snappy manner. 'The one with the large hands is Figgis, the one with the bulging eyes is Bloodeye, the one with the enormous nose that wobbles when he flicks it is Twistel. They are totally loyal, completely black-hearted and stupid enough to obey all my orders. Let me show you how stupid and completely under my thumbs they are.'

He crackled his knuckles. 'Take the tall one prisoner,' he shouted.

This was too much for me. I don't mean I leapt to rescue My Uncle: that was just going to have to wait. I grabbed the roller-skates, snatched the toasting-fork which Figgis had dropped while trying to keep hold of Uncle Joe, and was off down the passage before you could say 'Knife'. Somebody did say 'knife' about ten seconds later, but I was too far away to let it worry me. Poor Uncle Joe, though. I hope no one was going to cut him up into convenient one-inch cubes, suitable for stewing or frying, while my back was turned.

I remembered, just in time, to open the door before going through it, and was out on the beach and away up the hill as fast as the roller-skates would carry me.

Will things ever be the same again? Watch this space.

4

I am almost brave

I didn't stop until I was a long way up the hill, and
then I started to think what Brave people do at
times like this. They stand up straight; their voices
never tremble; their teeth gleam in the sunlight;
they don't trip over their shoelaces.

I took the roller-skates off, so I couldn't trip over
them now. Well it was a start, wasn't it? Someone
else could trip over them now. The big question
was: should I sit here on this rock, looking out to sea
and worrying, or should I DO SOMETHING?

Difficult. Maybe it was a trick question. Should I
try and answer something easier? If seven dogs can
bark for nine hours, how long can three dogs bark
for? That was no easier. It would be a lot better if I
was two people, then I wouldn't keep having to
make decisions. I might argue more, though. Especially now, when there's only one toasting-fork to
play with.

There was only one thing certain in these dangerous parts. If I went back to where I was, I'd be
captured and disposed of in a slow and painful way.
Even if I did find Uncle Joe, I might not get him out
of there. He might lose his glasses, or forget the way
out. He'd just have to look after himself for a

change. Meanwhile, I thought I'd better find some-one helpful, the sort who always has a pencil and a torch and a time-table.

I slung the roller-skates over my shoulder, and went off up the hill, thinking BIG brave thoughts. Well, thoughts anyway. It was a very good hill, all green, and lumpy, with great big huge moth-bites taken out of the sides. That was the faraway bit of it at least. The top bit was hidden in a large grey cloud, and the bit which I was squelching through was all ploughed up and planted with rows and rows of green potato plants with white and yellow flowers. It all looked wonderful, but there was nothing and nobody anywhere except these pota-toes.

Then I noticed a bit of this anywhere that wasn't planted with potatoes, and this was a forest. Well, a very small forest. Well, all right, ten trees, if you're so fond of arguing . . . And an amazing amount of green bushy things to stop you getting through the middle.

As I looked, I noticed a shape shuffling about inside, and a thin stream of smoke twisting out of the top of the trees. I walked round carefully, so as not to disturb the potatoes. Actually that wasn't the reason, I only walked round carefully so that the shape wouldn't see me. It had, though.

'Auuuuuuuuuooooom. And what be you doing of, young man?' squeaked the shape as I came closer.

51

'I'm coming towards you,' I said, because I was.

'Auuoooom. Mmm, yay, yay,' said the shape, and went back into the bushes. The smoke began to get thicker and I heard the shape coughing. It coughed with a deeper voice than it talked with. Maybe the smoke had something to do with that. And again, maybe not. It doesn't matter now.

I stuck my hand into one of the bushes to help myself through all the thorns. There was another squeak and the sound of branches breaking.

'Auuuuuuooooom, yay. I'm killed this time, and no mistake,' came the voice. 'I hope you'll be sorry when you see how dead I am. Mmm, dead, yes.'

I got through into the wood at last, and saw a small tubby man sitting on the ground, trying to get his left foot out of a very difficult looking trap.

'Arrr,' he said, when he saw me. 'Mmm, I'm caught in my own trap here, young man. You'd better try to get me out. I'll tell you though, mmm, mmm, 'tis a tricky one here.'

I looked at the trap. It wasn't very sharp, with great big iron jaws waiting to take your leg off, or wooden stakes to stick you through. But there was a lot of string and a lot of rope tied in knots round bent sticks. The string was red and covered in cardboard arrows.

The small tubby man cheered up when I began untying him with the help of the arrows. (The arrows seemed to show you how to untie all the knots.)

''Tis a trickster that I am,' he said as I reached the final knot. 'You should stay with me a while and I'll show you a trick or two. Yay, mmm.'

Every time he said 'Yay,' I noticed that he gave his right ear a tug, which accounted for it being a lot longer than the left one. And every time he said 'Mmm,' he fiddled with the earpieces of a small round pair of glasses that had no glass in them, and looked wise.

The last knot came undone, and he was free, but I wasn't. By now I was all tied up.

'Aaaauuooooom,' he said, leaping to his feet, ''tis you that is caught in the trap now, young man. Yay! That's why they call me Traplot. Traplot the

poacher. And I won't let you go till you tell me who you are and if you want to cut down any more of my trees. I can't live in the middle of the wood if there's no more wood left.'

As he said all this he trotted round behind me to look me up and down. I struggled with the knots I had just untied for him, and wondered how I had got caught up in all this.

He trotted back where I could see him, and a ray of sun caught some coloured letters on the sack he was wearing. *This sack holds 500 mangel wurzels,* they read. But it didn't. It was full of Traplot. Why didn't it say something more exciting like *Eat at Smoky Joe's Café* or *Read The Beano*? Or even *Read at Smoky Joe's Café* and *Eat The Beano*?

I told him I didn't have an axe, and that I couldn't do much to his trees with a toasting-fork. I didn't tell him about the other things the toasting-fork was supposed to do, just in case.

I waved the fork at him, to show what a friendly fork it was. He jumped, then rubbed his hands together with a chuckle and a rustle of sacking.

''Twas just a little joke', he said, 'and a very old joke, but a good joke all the same. Yay,' and he pulled on a long trailing piece of string that didn't seem to be part of the trap.

Before I could even sneeze (it was a very dusty wood), I was untied and looking at him face to face and eye to eye.

'Don't you worry about a thing,' he said. 'You just stick around with me and you might learn something.'

This seemed like a good idea, but I remembered I had to save the world from the AWFUL THING. I told him so.

'Have you?' he said. 'We all have to stop awful things from happening every day, and we don't go wandering around getting caught in other people's traps and disturbing their sleep. Unless 'tis a serious business?' I explained it all to him again, and he grabbed me by the hand and led me over to where the smoke was coming from. There, in a clearing ankle-deep and axle-deep in mud, stood an old black car FULL of sweet-papers.

'Isn't it a fine thing?' he asked proudly.

'Will it stop the world ending?'

'Nay, nay, but 'tis a fine thing, young man, a fine thing to see before the end of the world. A thing that has looked after me when I couldn't walk for being so frost-bitten. If I can get the engine to work I can take you away over the fields to see my friend the fortune-teller, to ask her what to do about all this trouble. I'm too busy here with my traps and my little tricks to stop the world ending.'

I scratched my head and let him get on with it. I hoped that the car was a bit faster than him.

The car didn't start, in fact it looked as if it wouldn't work at all.

Traplot got out of the driver's seat and looked at me.

' 'Tis a ferret that I need,' he said, ' a ferret to put

into the engine and chase out all the evils and weevils that are blocking up all the tubes.' He looked worried and had to wipe his brow, breathing heavily. Like this.... and like this........ and again like this....

'Why not put your hand up the exhaust-pipe?' I said, to hurry him up.

''Tis a very hasty young man,' he said, but knelt down and stuck his hand into the exhaust. The car shuddered a bit, as if he was the dentist.

Then with a great flourish, Traplot produced lots

of things out of the exhaust. There was a handful of dead leaves and an old onion and a few milk-bottle tops and a pair of gloves . . . and a live ferret, which ran away into the bushes.

As I looked away to follow the ferret, I noticed a very raggedy-looking crow flying over. It peered at me as if I was something off a WANTED poster, and settled on one of the ten trees.

We looked at each other, thinking EVIL THOUGHTS. The crow looked me up and down again, stuck up one claw, scratched its beak and flapped off. I had the feeling I *was* something off a WANTED poster. Perhaps the crow was something to do with Plover. It certainly looked like him.

I turned back to Traplot to hurry him up, but what I saw was odder than anything that had happened before. Traplot seemed to be stuck in the exhaust of his own car. It was trying to swallow him.

'Arr,' came a muffled squeak from inside the engine. 'I'm so stuck this time I don't think anyone can get me out. Don't you worry about me. I'll trick something out of this.'

'Where's the fortune-teller?' I asked.

'You just go across this field, young man, and you'll come to wherever it is that you want to go. And you go there and do what you have to do. Goodbye.'

'Goodbye,' I said and left him to it. I did think about pulling him out by the feet, but they had disappeared from sight. The engine had stopped smoking as well.

It was all too much, and I had to go. I did want to ask him about Boris the lion, if he really was in the shed. Perhaps the fortune-teller might know.

I set off across the field, as he told me, and went down a small dip into a hollow that I hadn't seen before. Mind you, as I had never been on this hill before, that wasn't surprising. There were potatoes planted here as well, but I noticed a small grey house first, because it was just about to fall down. As I walked up to it, it actually fell down. And there

in the middle of the rubble was a lady in a green cape in a rocking chair.

'Hmmm,' she said. 'I feel a terrible thing that is about to happen . . . a dark mysterious man is about . . . a dark mysterious man with fingers that crackle. . . .'

'Plover,' I thought.

'I can see other terrible things,' she went on. 'I can see the future happening now, I can see my house falling down.... and a stranger appearing with a pair of roller-skates.... This is all too much....'

I went over to her.

'I don't want to spoil your fun,' I said, slowly so as not to upset her, 'but I'm really here and your house really has fallen down.'

She took it well. 'Forgot to wind myself up,' she said, and swept her hair back with one hand. 'In fact that's not really true. I'm not very good at telling people's fortunes or seeing the future. That's why I live here where everybody knows what's going to happen just by looking at the sky. They only want to know if it's going to be sunny or rainy and they can do that themselves. I really wanted to be a mechanic and repair tractors. Your tractor hasn't broken down, has it?'

'No,' I said. 'I mean, I haven't got one.'

'Pity,' she said. 'Are you sure?'

'Yes,' I said. And I added quickly, 'Something terrible is going to happen.'

'Is it to do with tractors?' she said eagerly.

'No,' I said, starting to get excited. How could someone talk about tractors at a time like this? 'Do you know that if we don't do something to stop it, all the fishermen and all the farmers are going to have a big battle, and because they're not very good at fighting, they'll probably kill each other? And if they do kill each other, do you know what will happen?'

She didn't seem to be getting the point. After a couple of seconds, she replied, 'Well, I suppose there would be less tractors for me to repair . . . perhaps I'd have to keep chickens then . . .'

'What good would that be,' I yelped, 'if there was no more fish-and-chips left in the world?'

She saw what I meant and turned pale. I carried on explaining.

'Do you know a tall thin twisted man called Plover?' I asked.

'No,' she said, 'but I do know three very evil men called Figgis, Bloodeye and Twistel. Do you know what they did? They once burst all my supply of spare tyres. And they didn't use knives or pins — they used their teeth, and Figgis used his finger-nails as well. Even if I had repaired them, they would have been very odd tyres after that. I had to throw them all away.'

'This thin man Plover is behind it all,' I said, 'and he has Figgis, Bloodeye and Twistel to help him. You must help me.'

She saw what I meant and gathered up her crystal ball and her beads and her cards and coins and bamboo sticks. And a tool-box.

Then I remembered something. 'Where are all your chickens?'

'Traplot trapped them all and hid them some-where,' she said. 'He was helping me put my house back together the last time it fell down, when a bit fell off on to his head. He thought I was to blame, so he took my chickens.'

Wot a bunch, eh? The way they carry on up here. I should have asked a policeman before I talked to these strange folk. That's what my Mum would say, anyway. But there were no policemen around here.

By the time I had worked all this out, I realized that the fortune-teller hadn't really told me anything useful. She'd promised to help, but she hadn't told me a thing. Like for instance: where was the big battle going to take place? and what were they going to kill each other with? and where would we find someone to help us?

I fixed her with another HARD STARE, and asked her directly. She answered with another question.

'What do you call those metal things with wooden handles and lots of sharp points?'

'Pitchforks,' I said, and meant it too.

'Pitchforks,' she said, and narrowed her eyes, 'and spades. The fishermen will probably use boat-hooks and nets and those knives that they always have in their belts. And it'll most likely happen on the beach, because that lies between the two sides. And it'll all be very messy.'

I shuddered at the thought. Before she went on to answer the third question, I had a brilliant idea. Just as well really.

If the AWFUL BATTLE that we were trying to

stop was going to have a lot of people hitting each other with tools that all had wooden handles on them, then the best thing to do would be to find all the handles and burn them. And I had a toasting-fork that would do that, if I knew how to make it work. But to find that out I had to find Uncle Joe, unless I could find someone who *knew about machines* — which I had.

This made the idea all the more brilliant. And it wouldn't have anything to do with Uncle Joe (apart from having to rescue him). Look at the mess he'd made of things so far. Things that you're supposed to get right without really trying ... walking in a straight line ... not tripping over your own feet ... looking where you're going ... that sort of thing. He might only burn up one lot of handles, and give the other side an easy win. He might burn every-body up, including me. Worse, he might blow apart the strings that hold the world together, and fill the living-room with strange men. Then I'd really catch it from my Mum. 'I don't mind your friends,' she'd say. 'But I do mind their muddy boots. *You* don't have to clean the carpets round here.'

So we ought to DO something.

5

Van and his bulldozer (no onions)

Unfortunately there wasn't much happening at the moment. The fortune-teller hadn't yet worked out who we should ask, so we carried on walking *up* the hill instead of down, because it still might not be safe to go back without someone else.

As we walked on, I noticed a crow on a distant rock. It gave me one of *those* looks and went back to eating something hidden under its claws. I gave it a HARD STARE. It didn't seem to mind.

As we got closer, it got worried, and began to shift from one foot to the other. 'Caaark,' it went, and tried to peck casually at the end of its wing.

We stopped and watched it. It croaked again and gave another peck, this time under its wing. Then for no good reason, it flapped away on huge wings and was lost in the thick cloud which was now very close to us.

We both shuddered.

When we got up to the large grey cloud, we found out that the hill was really like one of those big ice-creams. One layer on top of another till you don't know where it ends. So above this lot of clouds was another lot of clouds ... and so on. The first lot of clouds had got a lot lower while we were wasting time on crows. In fact when we walked under them it was like walking into a bathroom full of cold steam. It was also a lot thicker than most sorts of porridge.

'HeEEEEeeeeee-EEEEEEEEEEEE-eeeeeelp,' came a voice from up in the cloud. 'Help, help!'

Something large like a boot fell down into the mud. I ran over to where it fell. It *was* a boot. I looked up to see where it had come from.

A large shape was flapping from side to side up in the cloud. As I watched it seemed to be going up . . . I called out to the fortune-teller but she was busy trying to find her crystal ball. She was fairly busy sneezing, as well, but only in threes. It could have been Morse code, but I didn't really notice. The shape in the cloud seemed to notice me.

'Don't just stand there blowing your nose and shuffling your feet!' it yelped. 'Catch hold of the end of the rope and pull me down.'

There *was* a rope and I pulled it. On the end was a very long thin man in a huge black coat, the sort of black coat that only a fat man would wear. This is what made him look like a balloon, because of the wind getting into it and blowing it out.

It wasn't too hard to bring him down to earth — it was rather like bringing a kite down. Perhaps he was one of the farmers who was so light that he had to be tied down in high winds, the way Uncle Joe had explained it to me.

'Thank you,' said the thin man when he was at the right end of his rope, and I had tied him down to stop it happening again. 'I'm one of those farmers who are so light that they have to be tied down in high winds, the way Your Uncle explained it to you. Pass my other boot.'

'Just a second,' I said, holding the boot out of reach. 'How do you know I've got an uncle, let alone the sort who explains things?'

'I've been watching you ever since you arrived. There was nothing else to do up here. Can I have my boots now?'

'I've only got one,' I said firmly. At this point, the fortune-teller arrived, blowing away huge slices of the cloud with her sneezes. At the sound of her sneezes, the man jumped.

'Was that the sound of cannons?' he said. 'Has

the battle started?'

'It was just me sneezing,' said the fortune-teller. 'It sounds more like an angry sea-lion than a gun, though.'

'Why are you arguing about the sound of her sneezes,' I shouted, getting excited again. 'And how do you know there's going to be a battle?'

The Chief Farmer decided yesterday,' said the man. 'My name's Van, because I always wanted to drive a van. But I don't have a van. I *do* have a tractor and a bulldozer.'

'Do you realize what will happen if there is a battle?' I said. 'Everyone will be killed. And worse still, there will be no more fish-and-chips in the world. Ever again.'

Van stood for a moment without saying anything. Then he MADE A DECISION. 'I'd better help you,' he said. 'But we'll have to be quick. Who else can we get to help us?'

'What about Boris the lion?' I asked him.

He pretended not to hear. Then he caught me looking at him. 'I'm pretending not to hear you,' he said. (I'll get to the bottom of this Boris business, just see if I don't. This whole adventure, as far as I can see is just a trick to keep me from finding out about Boris.)

'Right,' I said, and waved my hand in an IM-PORTANT GESTURE, like my cousin Ian who is something important in the Boy Scouts and supposed to be a LEADER AMONG MEN. 'What are we going to do? I mean what do we do first? And do we all stay together?'

'I should untie me first,' said Van who was beginning to get rather angry, sitting there in the mud with only one boot. 'Where's the other boot?'

The other boot was close by, in a puddle. In a very good puddle. I thought about trying to take it with me in case I needed it. Perhaps not.

I gave him his boot and untied him. They were very heavy boots, if you remember, to hold him down if the wind got too strong.

'Now,' he said, 'I'm going to get my bulldozer and take it down on the beach.'

'What for?' we both said.

'You can't fight on the beach if there's no beach to fight on,' he said.

He didn't explain why he had a bulldozer, or what use it would be to a potato farmer. I didn't ask, anyway. I was too busy working out how I could get a bulldozer for myself. When I become famous, I will have a bulldozer. When I get famous, I may not want to know about anyone else, especially if I get fat and have a bulldozer. YOU HAVE BEEN WARNED.

But at this point, Van was the only person to have a bulldozer. He was also very very thin and had a large shiny forehead. I never

actually caught him polishing it, but I'm sure he must do things like that when he's on his own.

He went off with the fortune-teller, because she wanted something to practise her engine-repairing on. Before he went, he told me where all the pitchforks and sharp things might be put before a battle. This was another thing he'd seen from up there in the clouds. Well, he hadn't actually seen the sharp objects, but he had seen a lot of to-ing and fro-ing earlier on that day down on the beach, which didn't happen every day. Because the Chief Farmer was a lazy man. He liked nothing better than to sit in a comfortable place and watch his potatoes grow. If someone a bit livelier had painted a wall, he might get out of his chair and watch the paint drying, but only if he felt like it.

So off went Van and the fortune-teller to carry the beach away and put it somewhere safe. They also promised to put it back safely where it belonged

when everything was over. They also promised to scoop up Plover, Figgis, Bloodeye, and Twistel if they saw them. They didn't say what they might do with them.

And I went off to rescue Uncle Joe, which I should have done a long while ago. I had the toasting-fork and my roller-skates. But how was I going to get through to the Chief Farmer and rescue anyone with that lot?

I wished again that there were two of me, possibly even three. Still, my feet were too busy being cold and wet to let me worry for too long about anything else. I kept kicking the mud off my shoes in case my Mum turned up suddenly. She does that, you know. I looked the toasting-fork up and down but there weren't too many buttons and none of them said what they were for. I pointed it at a puddle and pressed the first. Nothing.

I was about to press the second when I noticed that I was a bit close to the beach. Actually I didn't notice, it was my nose that noticed, because of the onions.

'What onions?' I thought. Now read on . . . .

6

Things look even better — or do they?

(Onions? What onions? You will have to wait.) I sneaked behind a rock and thought about my next move. Then I heard rustling noises and a lot of out-of-breath noises. The rock had put itself in the way so I couldn't see a thing.

The sounds became more strange: rustling plastic, and hissing, and a few lines of poems I'd never heard before.

A passing cloud threw a huge shadow over everything before going somewhere else more important. I slid closer. And a bit closer. And a bit closer again.

Peering around the rock, I noticed two men trying to stuff a large colourful thing into a black plastic sack. The colourful thing kept thumping them with its tail, as it didn't want to go into the sack.

I recognized the two men as Figgis and Twistel, because the one on the left had enormous hands and kept breaking off from what he was doing to flick the end of the other one's nose and then laughing a very wheezy laugh as he watched it wobble.

The colourful thing looked very like the python on my bedroom wall. In fact if it had been paper and hadn't kept reciting bits of poem, it *would* have been the python off my bedroom wall.

'*Bearded Fishlock sits in his den,*' it breathed,
'*Is his strength the strength of ten?*'

Figgis and Twistel both winced at this awful poem and tried to tie a knot in the poor animal to shut it up.

'*A doughnut is a triffic thing,*' it carried on,
'*A sugar-coated lordly ring,*
Made by men in crumpled coats,
Who work by night to earn their groats . . .'

That verse came to a sudden halt as Twistel stuffed another plastic bag into the python's mouth.

Time for action.

Untying the roller-skates I slid round the other side of the rock. The snake saw me and decided I was a good thing, since I wasn't joining in the GENERAL NASTINESS going on.

With a quick flick of an unusual muscle, it edged Figgis and Twistel backwards towards the rock. When they were almost touching it, I slipped a roller-skate under both their left feet and gave a huge shove. The python and I fell over backwards and the other two disappeared down the hill at a huge speed, shouting with surprise. After a few seconds there came a very loud splash, and a lot of gurgling.

I picked myself up and looked for the snake. I was thinking quickly, which I don't usually do. The snake was just the sort of thing to frighten everyone with and help rescue Uncle Joe with.

So far so good. But where had it gone? And did it like me? And did it care about the world ending in two hours' time?

I looked around for a while, but I still couldn't see a thing, let alone a snake. Then a loud whisper came from the top of the rock.

'*What happens if you kiss a fish?*' began the voice,
'*Do doctors come to patch your leg?*
Do gardeners planting rose and radish
Ask if you would like an egg?'

That sort of rotten dreadful poem could only come from the snake. I looked up and there it was, sunning itself on top of the rock, still half-wrapped in black plastic.

'Do pythons come all wrapped up like that round here?' I asked. 'Or are you just lazy?'

'I'm just lazy,' said the snake, and wriggled on the top of the rock to try and get the plastic bag off.

We looked at each other for a long time. A lot

more dark clouds went by in a hurry as if they didn't want to be mixed up in this sort of thing. By this stage, I didn't, either. I tried again.

'Why do you keep on reciting such awful poems?' I asked.

The snake began another poem.

I am old.
And my skin is cold.
And I am easily rolled
Into the lake.
I am the poem-snake.'

'That's a daft kind of snake to be,' I said.

'Yes, but I'm rather good at it, don't you think? It seems such a waste....'

'But the poems don't make sense.'

'Do you?'

'No.'

'Does anything around here?'

'There won't be much left of anything round here if we don't hurry,' I said. 'Do you know what's going to happen? Do you? I will tell you what is going to happen. All the farmers and all the fisher-

73

men are going to have a big battle down on the beach, and they will probably kill each other all over the place. And if there are no farmers to grow potatoes, and no fishermen to catch fish, how will the world make fish-and-chips? And what will we do when there's no fish-and-chips?'

'I'm not convinced,' said the snake. 'Perhaps I should tell you about life in the jungle, and how I came to be a poem-snake. Then I'll think about what you told me, and I might have a poem about it in a few weeks' time, if you'd care to wait.'

I was so angry that I couldn't speak, and the snake carried on talking.

'It's all because I used to get bored with eating goats, like all the other pythons. Then I used to lie around thinking up these WONDERFUL TRIF-FIC poems, and by the time I got out of that there wouldn't be any goats left anywhere. And I'd have to eat owls. Can you imagine it? All those claws and bones and beaks. I had to leave the jungle in the end. It's not that wonderful here because I have to eat eels, but you get used to them in the end.'

'Has this got anything to do with anything?' I said, giving him one of my kill-a-man-at-2,000-yards-looks.

The snake didn't like it. I began to get worried. Was he going to turn round suddenly and give me a BIG HUG and then eat me? He was being very friendly but he had a shifty look about the coils. He hadn't said anything about pythons eating people, though. Perhaps no one told him that they sometimes do. Well I wasn't going to be the first.

'Are you going to help me, or aren't you?' I said angrily.

'Will it mean getting up and not sleeping as much as I want? And having to move fast and all those sort of things?'

'It's only for a couple of hours.'

'I do like to sleep as much as possible. Sometimes even more than that.'

'If you don't help me, there won't be any time any more for going to sleep and that sort of thing.'

'O. . . . all right. But only if you drag me along in this nice plastic bag. It's warmer that way.'

There was no more to be said. The snake had me in a tight corner, if he knew what tight corners were.

I tugged on the bag, which was amazingly heavy.

'Can't you wriggle a bit?' I asked. 'Just to make it easier for me to pull this bag along?'

'Only if you don't drag me over any lumpy bits.'

So I agreed to drag him over smooth bits only, and let him say his useless poems every ten minutes if he felt like it.

I couldn't really go through the front door of the Chief Farmer's cave. They might recognize me. I'd have to go round through the side door. That, if you remember, was the door that Plover took us through in the wheelbarrow, the door that led to the pickling plant. There might be other doors and tunnels to lead me in the right direction when I'd got inside. But what *was* the right direction? Maybe I could make it up as I went along, the way I do at school.

I set off down the hill again, looking round for enemies.

By the time I was at the bottom, Figgis and Twistel were out of the sea. I could tell that by the wet footprints leading over to the main door. They also left the roller-skates behind to dry. Since they were the sort with plastic wheels that don't go rusty, I picked them up and slipped in through the side door of the palace.

It was very dark inside. I couldn't see anybody, and nobody could see me. The walls still felt like a lizard's bathroom. This time they smelt a bit like it too, but there wasn't time for that sort of thing at the moment.

The snake had managed to fall asleep, so I didn't have to worry about a poem coming out at the wrong moment. I did wish I could sneeze a few times without it mattering. I wondered if the snake had any longer poems, the sort that have middles and ends, not just beginnings. But they might be even worse.

A lump in my path woke the snake up again. There was a lot of hissing and some more poem:

'... *the strength of ten?*
Yes it was, but how could he know?
Thinking of naught but slow-quick-slow,
Snorting like a Pacific loco ...'

At least the snake had the sense to whisper, but it was pretty bad all the same.

'Can you see in the dark?' I asked.

'No, but I can hear better. Let me out of this bag and follow me.'

This sounded fishy. 'Stay in the bag,' I said, 'but stick your head out. Think what might happen if you get caught again.'

He stuck his head out. 'Nothing out there,' he said. 'Another poem?' Well at least he asked.

'No! Back into your bag.'

We went on down the tunnel, past the pickling vat where Uncle Joe and I nearly got pickled before.

I stopped. It might be an idea to let the python out and make him do something. He might get angry sleeping in that bag all the time. So I turned him loose and asked him to sort the tunnel out. This seemed to please him and he went off, humming softly to himself.

77

In a few minutes he was back. 'It bends round here a lot,' he said. 'And a bit further up, it branches into two. One branch goes uphill, the other downhill.'

'We'll go downhill', I said, hoping that there wasn't anything nasty at the other end. The tunnel going down had a dot of light at the end of it, I noticed. The python said his eyes hurt and crawled back into the bag.

Suddenly I heard footsteps approaching. Still thinking quickly I drew the plastic bag up in front of me and hid behind it.

A shape shuffled past, singing noisily. I peeped at it as it went past. From the bulging eyeballs, I thought this must be Bloodeye. It was. In one hand he carried a mop, and in the other a bucket of small fish.

I listened carefully. From a long way off, possibly the end of the tunnel, I heard strange deep rumblings and the sounds of squirting, as if someone was playing with a large hose. I suddenly felt that this wasn't the place to be. No one would keep prisoners down at the bottom of this tunnel and feed them on fish. Perhaps it was a passing herd of seals?

No time to work it out. We turned round, and tried the other branch.

This branch got lighter as we went along it, but the floor was messier. There were old potatoes everywhere, with little white and green shoots growing out of them.

All of a sudden I smelt frying. It seemed to come from a hole in the rock. I sneaked over, and held the bag in front of me as I went. That way, someone passing would think I was a piece of darkness. The hole wasn't very big. I tried to look through it, but saw nothing. One of us would have to go through the hole, and I was too big. Just in case there was something nasty like a 5,000 foot drop below the hole, I stuck my hand through. I felt a slope running down. This must be some sort of pipe, I thought.

I woke the python, let him tell me about *Bearded Fishlock* once again, and then told him what he had to do. I was worried that someone might come back along the tunnel, Bloodeye for instance. They must all be busy somewhere else. We would have to do more than we thought. And do it quicker too.

I looked round for another way down. After a lot of slime and darkness, I found a doorway, with steps leading down. The floor seemed a long way away, and it was all downwards. The frying smell was everywhere. As I got lower, the darkness stopped being very dark, and was just very very smoky instead. I wished I could sneeze again.

I peered through the smoke and steam and saw Uncle Joe in a TIGHT CORNER. The evil Plover was strutting up and down smiling an evil smile at Uncle Joe, who was hanging over a large pan of boiling oil. Each time Plover turned round he

79

crackled the joints of his fingers.

Uncle Joe didn't seem to be very worried, though. In fact he seemed the way he always seemed, except without the pipe.

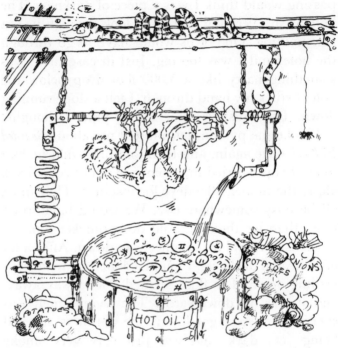

'Now,' said the evil Plover, 'I want you to tell me exactly what you're doing here, and why and where and how much of whatever you carry in your pockets. If you don't tell me, you will be lowered into the boiling oil that I've been heating up for the last three-quarters of an hour. It's very hot and you will be burnt to a crisp, hur, hur.' And crackled his finger joints again.

Uncle Joe shook his head, and blew a fly away from his left eye. Plover didn't like this and flicked his little head from side to side.

'I'm warning you,' he said, and crackled again. Everyone shuddered, even the python. It was a good thing that the python shuddered, because then I could see where he had got to. By this stage, the python was hanging from an iron girder in the ceiling and was pretending to be a yo-yo. I flashed him a FIERCE LOOK, which he noticed, and then he came slinking along the girders and pipes which seemed to be everywhere. I didn't have time to notice these pipes and things in the ceiling, because I was angry with the python.

'*Plover the thin*,' he began,
'*Whose heart is made of tin....*'

I didn't let him finish. 'Is about to fry My Uncle in oil,' I interrupted. 'So stop him with your coils.' He understood immediately.

While he went off to DO HIS STUFF, I hurried down the last of the steps, and hid behind the black plastic bag. I was now on the floor of the frying cave. I went over towards where Plover was, thinking that he couldn't see me, because I couldn't see him. This was a mistake. I mean if that was true, blind people would be invisible, wouldn't they?

Plover rushed over, as if he had been expecting

81

me. This time he clicked his teeth and his heels as well as his knuckles. I expect the oil that he was heating up shuddered at that.

'Just in time,' he said. 'Just in time to make two. I thought you'd be back to rescue Your Uncle. Those people you met up on the hill weren't much use to you, were they? Never expect anything from the people who live on the hill. They'll all end up horribly fried like you and Your Uncle.'

'It must be the crows,' I said. He laughed.

'Put those roller-skates down and come here. It's no good trying to stand in my way.'

I bent down and threw a roller-skate at him, and as he ducked, several feet of angry python tied a knot around him. The snake then slithered up the wall in a snaky sort of way, tied himself to a beam, and began to yo-yo Plover. After a few minutes Plover began to look rather ill, so I asked him how to set Uncle Joe free.

'I shall never tell you,' he began. The snake began to work at double speed. 'Pull the red lever,' he said quickly. The snake, having a kind heart, went a bit slower. I pulled the red lever. There was a great whirring noise, and the vat of hot oil moved gracefully into a far corner.

'What now?' I asked.

'There's a green button marked D for down', called out Uncle Joe, who was enjoying the sight of Plover being used as a yo-yo.

I wasn't sure about this. Uncles can be wrong, you know.

'There really is a green button, marked D,'gurgled Plover. 'Press it.'

I pressed it, and Uncle Joe came down rather gracefully on the end of a long chain. I got him out of the ropes that he was tied up with and stopped the machine. (There was a red button marked S for stop.)

Then Uncle Joe and I explained to each other all that had happened since we got split up. Then we had to do it all over again because it had been too fast the first time. After that we tied up Plover with a sticky old end of rope and left him in a dark corner to see how it felt to be on the wrong end for a change. We had to burn up all the sharp things' handles before it was too late, and then do something about the fishermen. And then.... And then nothing. We just had to do it. I mean what would happen if there wasn't any fish-and-chips?

I was full of other questions to ask Uncle Joe, but that would have to wait. We both hustled the python back into the bag and rushed out and away down the passage. We must have taken the wrong turning, because we ended up at the passage going down. Still, there couldn't be so many people down here, so it was a lot less dangerous.

For some reason I couldn't understand Uncle Joe then put on the roller-skates and shot off down the tunnel on his own. Perhaps he knew this from before. I still couldn't work out why he was so dreamy all the time and then kept doing these weird things, which came right in the end. And what about Boris the lion?

I sat down in the passage and worried and worried and worried. The python sat down beside me and tried to cheer me up with things which he said were 'Ever so well liked in the jungle.' If I'd had knees nine foot across, I'd have spanked him, really I would.

Why do I have to have such an unlikely uncle? So much trouble. So few bacon sandwiches to take my mind off it. I wonder if pythons are good to eat?

7

Will there be a Chapter 10?

'You're not talking much', said the snake. 'It makes me nervous. Say something. Talk. Say anything.'

'mmmMMMMbbrr,' I replied. That isn't a magic word. It's just something that you say when you're trying to talk through a mouthful of your own knuckles. The snake wasn't the only one who wasn't comfortable.

'sspppbbblllo,' I went on.

Was the snake going to do a nasty turn on me? Was I being kind to animals, the way I should? My hands got sticky and my nose got sweaty, like nobody's business. (Who wants a sticky sweaty business anyway?)

I got up and carried on down the tunnel, thinking in-between sort of thoughts about everything. The snake slithered after me, and we slithered along together. I soon gave it up, the thinking not the slithering, I mean. I like slithering. Don't you?

All this idle chit-chat and arky-malarky didn't really get us anywhere fast. But then it was a very dark tunnel, and not very interesting to talk about. It's not as if they have holiday postcards of the place to send off to your friends. HAVING NICE TIME. WISH YOU WERE HERE. WORLD ABOUT

TO END IN TWO HOURS FROM LACK OF FISH-AND-CHIPS.

'And what is the thing at the end of the tunnel?' I asked the snake.

'The crock of gold at the end of the rainbow?' he whispered. 'Mrs Golda Endcork, bowing in the rain? An old crock on the brow of a gain?' I told him to keep that to himself.

Before he had time to argue, we'd both bumped into something. It was dark and warm and a lot blacker than the rest of the darkness, and a lot shapelier as well. It was rumbling in a particular way that made everything else rumble with it. Imagine a thumb as big as possible. That's what it looked like.

I still couldn't decide what it was. Perhaps Uncle Joe had eaten the wrong kind of mushroom, and blown up like a balloon. Unlikely. What Uncle Joe ate usually had jam on it. It must be . . . a whale.

It was in fact the whale that belonged to the King of the Fishermen! This might be a GOOD THING. But what was Uncle Joe up to down here?

A smaller dark shape appeared from under the whale. It grabbed me by the neck and told me to give the whale a big push from this end. It must have been Uncle Joe because it was smoking a pipe.

I grabbed his ear and whispered something about the python into it. He coughed. The python coughed. We all coughed. I think it must have been

the smoke from the pipe.

We all got behind the whale and gave it a mighty push. It quivered. So did everything else, and down came most of the ceiling. So who needs a ceiling? Who needs a bruise on the head either? Owwww!

The whale seemed to get the idea and began to flobber its way back down the tunnel, with us close behind. The farmers up above must have noticed something by now. I listened out for following footsteps. Nothing.

Stepping lightly over heaps of greasy old bricks, we followed the whale as it wriggled its way down the ruins of the tunnel.

'How do we know where this tunnel goes?' I asked.

'Because I went down it on roller-skates, that's

how,' said Uncle Joe. 'Now shut up and carry on pushing.'

'Listen,' hissed the snake.

'We ARE being followed,' said My Uncle.

'It's just an echo,' I said, hoping to hear the echo of my own words. I heard footsteps instead. And a nasty sort of breathing that turned my blood to glue.

My nose started to run. I started to run. We all started to run, as fast as the whale would let us. Not very fast. Perhaps this is why people don't keep whales for pets. They'd keep getting stuck in tunnels with them. This is why they have to live in the sea and get hunted. Not fair really.

Suddenly we all fell over the whale and each other. The voices came nearer, and began making evil suggestions. There was a creaking noise from the tunnel, because it had got too narrow for the whale.

I had an idea, in fact everyone had the same idea at the same moment, and we all gave the whale a big shove. The whale in turn flapped his fins (or her fins, I'm not sure which).

The first push was no use nor was the second. Meanwhile the voices and footsteps were only just round the next corner. I could almost smell their feet. We all breathed in and gave ONE LAST PUSH. Hello, Plover, Figgis and Twistel: goodbye, Plover, Figgis and Twistel. PUuuuUUSH and then CRASH!

And then we were through into a sandy cave. In front of us waves lapped over the rocks and sand of the beach. Behind us five million tons of rubble came down and blocked the way back. We were safe, sort of, for the time being.

This made us all very cheerful, and Uncle Joe passed round oranges from a paper bag. Oranges make me sneeze, so I gave mine to the whale. The whale took no notice. Perhaps it was all that fish that Bloodeye brought. The whale was still making deep noises, somewhere between a cow and a bass guitar, only better. I could feel the sound in my belly, which is very large.

Still humming, the whale lumbered down the beach and disappeared quickly into deep water like the soap in the bath. We were all too busy with the orange peel to worry about that, until we realized that we could have used the whale to stop the fishermen (my idea), or to dig up the beach (Uncle Joe's idea), or to find some nice juicy eels to eat (the python's idea). And where was Van and his bulldozer? And why was all this beach still here?

In all the excitement, I noticed that Uncle Joe had lost his glasses. He hadn't noticed, and was walking around without tripping over things. Perhaps he didn't really need them.

Uncle Joe interrupted all this thinking. 'Perhaps we should give the whale back to the King of the Fishermen,' he said, lighting another pipe.

The python coughed politely. Then it coughed again, not so politely. At last it had to be taken away and given a large amount of water, to stop it choking.

'At least no one ever did that in the jungle,' he said, when he could speak properly again.

'Whence came this Fishlock?

On fat white feet the gypsies brought him.

Had they duped him, tricked him, bought him?'

I let him get away with that one. It had been very strong smoke. I left him breathing DEEPLY AND EVENLY, and went off to argue with Uncle Joe.

'We can't give the whale back,' I said, 'because he isn't ours, and he isn't here.'

'Yes,' replied Uncle Joe, and then added, 'possibly,' just to show that he didn't agree too much with anything.

I was about to make a few UNPLEASANT REMARKS when the whale came back and blew a lot of water over everyone, just to be fair about it. This *proves* that big fat things (whales and elephants) remember better than small thin things. This is another good reason for me to get really really fat one day. About the middle of next week, I hope. I'm not sure whether it's better to become famous first, though.

Uncle Joe made another suggestion. This time his idea was to take the whale back to the King of the Fishermen, and stop him going out to fight. This might not be a BRILLIANT IDEA, only half of one perhaps (BRILL ID), but it did take care of the fishermen, and what we were going to do with them. What's more, Uncle Joe promised to take the python with him.

So off they went. I could see the python's lips saying the words '*Bearded Fishlock sits in his den....*' when Uncle Joe let out another puff of smoke, like a steam-roller. The python coughed a lot and said nothing. Perhaps Uncle Joe did know what he was doing sometimes.

I sat down on a rock and started worrying about what to do next. I picked up some of the orange peel and put it into a bag. Then I put the bag into another bag and hid it behind the rock, hoping that my Mum hadn't seen me, or didn't find out.

Then I waited and I waited and I waited. I counted up to 10,000 a few times, and I even tried to remember some of the python's poems, and at last... I heard a strange rumble in the distance.

I got up and looked, and there in the distance was a large bulldozer zooming down in my direction. It didn't stop and say Hello, it just broke down the front door of the cave where the Chief Farmer lived.

I ran all the way there and followed them in. I heard feet running away in all directions leaving piles and piles of roller-skates behind. And there was this amazing smell of onions. Yes, onions. These are the onions that I made you wait all these pages for. Was it worth it? Now read on.... The smell was so amazing that it laid the seagulls flat for about ten minutes. But we couldn't find anyone to catch or anyone to rescue. The whole of the cave where the Chief Farmer had been was empty.

Van stopped his bulldozer. There was a long silence. Everywhere.

This could only mean one thing. If no one was up this tunnel waiting to hit us all on the head with something knobbly, they must have gone some- where else, maybe outside, to beat each other up and the fishermen as well. Perhaps they had already started, perhaps it was already over. Perhaps there was no more fish-and-chips left in the whole world, and the world had ended.... We still had a lot to do to stop the AWFUL THING happening.

Van started up the bulldozer again, and went on to find somewhere to turn round in.

As he rounded a corner, we all noticed a gleam of light from under a doorway in the rock. We stopped and put our ears to the rock.

At first there was nothing, but after a while a slow sort of buzzing began, like a crowd whispering to each other. The whispering grew louder and turned into clapping. Then someone stopped the clapping and began to speak in a voice that echoed round and round the room behind the door of rock. Perhaps it wasn't a room, perhaps it was a huge great hall with enormous great beams at the top and rotten greasy smelly ropes hanging down from the beams, like the gym at school.

'You all know why we've come here,' said the voice.

'Here ... here ...' went the echoes.

'Before we go to find our weapons, we must work out our plan of battle. This means that I am going to tell you what to do. And what I say, goes, OK?' The voice belonged to Plover, but it wheezed a bit. He must have swallowed a lot of dust when the tunnel fell down on him.

'First,' he went on, 'you all go out to the beach and pick up the SHARP PITCHFORKS and DANGEROUS SPADES stacked up there. Then you line up into three lines, and I want them to be straight this time!'

'And then?' said a voice from the back of the room.

'And then?' said Plover, 'And then? You mean you don't know what to do then? You're very lucky I don't have you pickled for being so stupid. Or thrown off the cliff into the sea. Remember, angels can fly but not with concrete boots on! And things float in the sea, but not with ENORMOUS GREAT BIG HEAVY CHAINS round their necks! When the fishermen get out of their boats, you take up your weapons and drive them back into the sea WHERE THEY BELONG!'

There was a lot of cheering at this, and they

93

began to sing a song with not many words and a lot of stamping and shouting.

We looked at each other and shot backwards down the tunnel. I looked at the toasting-fork and hoped it would do its stuff properly. I also hoped that Uncle Joe would come back in time to tell me how to make the thing do its stuff properly. I even wished that the python had stayed behind to help.

Luckily Van had a CLEAR HEAD.

'The first thing to do', he said, 'is find the weapons.'

As his bulldozer had knocked down most of the caves where someone could hide a lot of SHARP PITCHFORKS and DANGEROUS SPADES, it only left the beach. There was a lot of beach, though.

Where could we start? Then the fortune-teller had a BRILLIANT IDEA. I could tell she'd had an idea because she stopped worrying and smiled and shook her beads a bit.

'Maybe Plover and his friends were chasing you down the tunnel when in fact they *weren't* chasing you.'

This was either very clever or just plain daft. I waited to see if there was any more of the idea.

'What I mean,' she said, 'is that maybe Plover and all that lot were going to hide all the weapons at the end of the tunnel and just managed to put them all down and run away before the roof fell in. They might not know that it was you who made the roof fall in by pushing the whale out. We've got to go back in to catch Plover and his evil assistants. If we follow them, they might lead us to where they've hidden the weapons. Jump on the bulldozer.'

We all jumped on, the fortune-teller, that is, and me. Van was already on the bulldozer, grinning all over his face and a bit of the back of his head as well.

Van had got the bulldozer out of the farmers' cave. 'Climb aboard,' he said. So we did. Soon we were shooting along the beach, digging it up in all directions as we went. We both had to hold on tight to the bulldozer so as not to fall off. Van didn't say 'Great idea,' or anything, he just steamed towards the cave and started to heave the rocks away with the bulldozer. He must be fond of that bulldozer, I thought.

Now that the dust had settled, we saw that the rocks that had fallen down weren't blocking the way completely, so we might be able to get in after a bit of heaving.

In the middle of all this heaving, Van turned round and grinned at both of us. 'I'm fond of my bulldozer,' he said, and he really meant it.

Just then the bulldozer got stuck on a rock and we had to go backwards. There was just enough room for me to squeeze into the cave past some rocks, so I did. I took the fork with me as well.

Inside the cave, there was a very fishy sort of smell. Luckily I didn't have far to look, since there wasn't much light. Against the wall some kind person had made two neat piles of things-to-hit-

people-with. Thirty seconds later, one unkind person (ME) had turned the whole lot to ashes with the toasting-fork. The fork didn't work at first, so I had to practise on some of the moss and green things that were growing everywhere in the cave, pressing all the buttons in a different order. When it did work, though ... VOOM! Ashes.

I hurried back to the bulldozer and we backed out of the cave and hid behind a rock. It was the same rock that I'd hidden the orange peel behind, I noticed. I picked it up, just in case my Mum turned up, and hid it under the fortune-teller's toolcase, which was stuck on the back of the bulldozer.

We waited and waited, and after a while we heard the sound of boots coming down the tunnel. A lot of farmers ran out on to the beach, chased by an angry man in a broad black hat. Who was this angry man? He must have been a quite important farmer to be so angry. The angry man was holding up a handful of ashes and muttering at them. Then he threw his handful of ashes at the other farmers and yelled, 'The pitchforks have all been burned. What are you going to DO about it?'

The other farmers looked at their boots, and didn't say much. One decided to be brave and said quietly, 'We could use the metal bits of the pitchforks for something.'

'They've all been melted,' said the angry farmer

in the big black hat. And, to show how angry he really was, he threw his hat on the sand and jumped on it.

Then he finally lost all his temper. 'Go and find Mr Plover,' he yelled.

As he hadn't told anyone in particular to go and find him, all the farmers ran back inside, kicking sand and dust everywhere. The angry man went back indoors, and Van hopped on to the bulldozer and sealed the doorway behind him.

Somewhere in the distance, a large black shape appeared in the sea, with something like a funnel on its back. It was like a funnel (the something, I mean) because there was lots of thick black smoke coming out of it. Somewhere in a different part of the distance, a lot of boats appeared, all heading for the beach. It was the fishermen on their way to the battle.

We still had a lot to do to stop the world from ending.

There was a shout and a lot of digging and scrabbling noises in the cave. Van revved up the bulldozer and zoomed off down the sand.

I took another look at the boats out at sea. I saw a lot of men in yellow oilskins waving their knives in the air. Some of them were also waving long poles with hooks on the end. We still had to stop them fighting. Nobody else could do anything to stop it. Unless the bottom of the sea suddenly vanished.

That would make people sit up and take notice. Especially the sea.

As these horrible thoughts ran through my head, a large flock of crows wheeled overhead and landed on a lump of rock somewhere up the cliff. I shuddered. We all shuddered, even the bulldozer.

I turned and looked round at the beach. We still hadn't dug up very much of it. We wouldn't have the time to do much more, either.

Just as I was thinking this, the same thought hit Van.

'Ouch,' he said, rubbing the bruise where the thought had hit him.

He stopped the bulldozer. He then jumped down, helped the fortune-teller down, helped me down, and took a telescope out of his pocket.

'This is a very useful telescope,' said Van.

I didn't know what to say, so I said nothing.

'If I didn't carry this telescope around with me all the time, I wouldn't know what was happening when I get blown away up into the clouds.'

There was a lot of splashing going on out at sea. Van had a look and passed the telescope to me. I took the telescope, put it to my eye, saw nothing, opened the telescope and closed my eye, saw nothing, closed my other eye and the telescope, saw stars when I bumped my head, opened both eyes and the telescope and at last made out the thing that was doing all the splashing.

In fact it was My Uncle Joe, smoking all his pipes at once to confuse the enemy. And he was riding on the back of the whale. Help was arriving just in time!

A large crow, that I had seen before, landed on the end of the telescope. It began to look down its

beak at me. I tried to look away, but it started pecking at my fingers. There were crows pecking at Van's fingers, too, and we climbed onto the bulldozer. Van started the engine to try and escape. But we were not to get away. We hadn't gone more than a few yards when the ground began to move under the bulldozer.

'A trap,' I thought.

But this was not any old ordinary trap. This was worse than Traplot and his string. A huge hole appeared in the ground and the bulldozer disappeared into it. And we went down with the bulldozer, bringing down loads of old seaweed and fishy-smelling things on top of us.

'Cheer up,' I said to myself. 'Something worse might happen, with an even more evil pong.'

Worse than the onions, I mean.

8

Not the beginning. But is it the end?

So there we were, Van, the fortune-teller and me, feeling very down. As down as we could feel, because we were right at the bottom of this hole in the ground. It was going to be difficult to get out of this one, we all thought together. And the battle might still happen now that we were out of the way and not able to DO anything.

Then came the big surprise. Machines started humming and whirring *underneath* all the seaweed and things at the bottom of the pit. Before we knew what had happened to us, a huge spring-loaded

platform shot us out of the pit and high up into the

air. Someone was taking no chances with us. Just in case we HAD found a way of climbing out of the pit, we'd got shot up into the air out of the way.

But where were we going to land? I looked down, and the ground seemed a long way away. It also had the kind of bumps and sharp bits that are NOT GOOD TO FALL DOWN ON. Not from a long way up without a parachute. I shut my eyes and waited for the crash.

It came rather quicker than it should have done. I opened my eyes. Instead of landing like a lot of strawberry jam on the rocks by the sea, we'd landed in a very squelchy field near the edge of the cliff. This was a GOOD THING, and a lot better than being all smashed up. But we still had to stop this battle. How were we going to do that?

I looked out to sea. Uncle Joe and the whale had come closer. I waved at him. He was about to wave back, when huge amounts of seagulls appeared from all round and got in the way. They must like eating whatever it was that smelt so awful.

All at once, for no good reason, the whale surfaced in among the seagulls. Uncle Joe must have got left behind somewhere, because he wasn't there at all. Nor was the python.

QUICK AS A FLASH the whale blew a huge great spout of water. Really huge. Huge enough to blow the seagulls right into next week ... and to catch the bulldozer and us with it by the underneath

... and lift us ... off the cliff and hold us up like a ping-pong ball on the top of a fountain ... which was all very well till you think what happens when a whale runs out of water to hold us up with. Yes, you're right — you come down again.

I felt sick again and shut my eyes and put my hands over my ears.

After a long time I dared to look up again. I felt like a person who has gone down to the ground floor in a fast lift and then taken an even faster lift to the ninety-seventh floor.

We were still on top of the cliffs, but this bit wasn't so high. There was also a steepish slope leading down to the beach. Well, at least it led

SOMEWHERE. Van looked rather pale but he was still smiling. The fortune-teller was putting all her beads into the tool-box, along with her coins, sticks and bits and pieces for telling fortunes.

Van tried to start the bulldozer. It coughed a lot, but wouldn't start. After a while it wouldn't even cough.

There was a long silence.

We were still in a mess, the world could still come to a NASTY END at any minute, and I was fed up with being a hero and having to sort it out. Mind you I hadn't done anything a hero would do. Except wanting to shout HELP! in a very loud voice and then hide in a corner. I'm sure heroes must do that sometimes. Maybe a whole load of heroes get together and do it in a darkened room with lots of corners to hide in.

The fishermen's boats began to get close enough to climb out of. I craned my neck to see what the farmers were up to.

I couldn't see any farmers anywhere. They must have been stuck in the cave. This might be the safest place for them at the moment. At least they stood no chance of being hurt by the fishermen in there — and if they weren't too clumsy, not hurt by each other as well.

A loud clatter from down below made me look down. It was Figgis barging his way out on to the beach from the tunnel, carrying three rocks on his huge stomach. Behind him came Twistel, peeling an apple with his long fingernails, and flicking the end of his nose from time to time. They both looked behind them, but no one followed them out.

'We're stuck in the doorway,' said a voice at the back.

Figgis reached into an enormous pocket and brought out a large grease-gun. He then went back into the cave, leaving Twistel to eat his apple.

I looked out at the nearest boat. There was a long green flag fluttering from the mast, even though I couldn't see any wind anywhere. And where was Uncle Joe?

I looked back. Twistel had finished his apple. He flicked the core in the air, and cut it in pieces with a few strokes of his nails. The seagulls, back from the middle of next week where the whale had blown them, caught all the pieces before they hit the ground.

I had an AWFUL THOUGHT. Perhaps the farmers would start to throw rocks instead of using pitchforks. And what about all the bottles that get washed up on beaches? And the oil? They might boil it up and throw it over the fishermen.

I took another look at the flag. It was wriggling rather a lot for a flag. And flags don't usually flicker their tongues in and out like that. At least, not where I come from, they don't.

I leaned forward and pointed. No one took any

notice, because Van and the fortune-teller were busy tinkering with the engine.

I looked out to sea. The green thing on the mast was definitely a python. THE python, the one I wasn't sure about. But I still couldn't see Uncle Joe. He must have fallen into the sea somewhere. I shall be in all sorts of trouble if I don't bring him home again, I thought.

The fortune-teller leapt up, greasy to the elbows, and got back into her seat on the bulldozer.

'It won't start unless we all push it,' she said. 'It's got water in the engine.' She'd even read the fortune of the bulldozer from its tracks, so she must have been right.

We got behind it and pushed. I even tried to dry the engine out with the toasting-fork, but it still wouldn't start. Then we remembered that if the bulldozer started in the direction we were pointing it, it would go over the cliff. We decided that this wasn't a GOOD THING.

But the bulldozer was too heavy to turn round when the motor wasn't working. It seemed that we were really stuck, and not just in the mud.

I took a deep breath, and looked down on to the beach. Van and the fortune-teller got stuck into the engine again, this time using one of Van's socks as a sponge.

As I watched, the evil Bloodeye (the one with the bulging eyes) trotted round a corner with several

106

sacks of onions over his shoulder. This looked serious.

I walked off quickly and tried to find a way down the cliff. I did find one, but it was very crumbly, and I had to walk slowly with bent legs.

As I started to come down, the beach began to fill up with farmers, all of them dobbed and dabbed with spots of grease. They grabbed handfuls of the onions which, by the smell of them, were very old and very bad. One or two rubbed grease into the onions to make them fly better.

I squeezed the toasting-fork and wondered what to do with it.

The fishermen, meanwhile, had been keeping a good look-out, and when they noticed all these goings-on on the beach, they slowed down their boats and stopped just out of range. Then they moved the boats into a big half-circle. What was going on?

It looked as if a battle would soon be going on. The fishermen were all lined up on one side in their boats, and the farmers were lined up along the beach with rocks and onions and anything that they could find to throw.

The evil Plover had appeared as well, on the farmers' side of things. He wasn't worried about being recognized by the fishermen, either. I could only make him out in the crowd because he was sitting on Figgis' shoulders. The Chief Farmer was also sitting on someone's shoulders, two people's shoulders in fact. But he'd chosen two short people, so no one could see him or work out where his orders were coming from. This meant that Plover was doing all the ordering about, which he had been from the start, if you ask me.

Although there was a lot going on on both sides, no one had started fighting yet.

I noticed a tall man in a green hat at the end of the line, who couldn't wait to throw his onion and was going to throw it before the order was given. I could tell this because he kept swinging his arm round in practice throws and growling things through clenched teeth.

At last he couldn't wait any longer. Drawing back his arm, he threw the onion out nearly as far as the boats. Several others joined in, who must have been

brothers, because they all had the same beard.

Quick as a flash I aimed the fork and blasted the onions to ashes. Huge coils of smoke rose into the air and hid everything from everything else.

Then I wriggled down the cliff a bit further till I was about twenty feet from the beach, and hid behind a rock.

There was a loud humming noise above my head, but I couldn't see in all the smoke. No one else took much notice of it, since there was a lot of running around and confusion among the farmers.

I wondered if the bulldozer was working properly again. And if the bulldozer was working, what were Van and the fortune-teller going to do with it? It might not be the bulldozer. The noise and smoke might be Traplot the poacher in his old black car. Still, I had too much to worry about here without thinking about what was going on up on top of the cliffs. I wished I'd had Van's telescope, though.

As the smoke cleared, I saw that the boats had moved out of the half-circle into a long line.

The farmers were getting ready to throw rocks. Plover was just saying, 'One, two, three THR. . . .' when a wave appeared from nowhere and swallowed up the beach.

This stopped the farmers doing very much, but the fishermen didn't do anything either. They seemed just as surprised. The wave disappeared, as mysteriously as it had come and some of the boats at the back began to move away slowly. They were soon noticed, and given A SHARP TALKING TO.

The boats moved back out of range again and this time began to go round in a huge circle. The farmers, in the meantime, were piling up rocks, in case another wave came to bother them.

Since everyone was out of range of everyone else, they had to shout insults instead of getting down to any serious kind of fighting. This was a GOOD THING, I thought. It would be a waste if they all killed themselves now, after all our running around to try and stop them. In fact it would be a waste if they did it at all.

'Who made my bicycle tyres go flat?' yelled a farmer.

'Who blocked my funnel with potato peelings?' yelled back a fisherman.

'You lot sawed my fork handle in half, and that's why I stuck it into my foot,' yelled another farmer, lifting up a foot in a bandaged welly.

'Where's the King's whale been for the last ten days?' yelled the fishermen.

And so it went on for ten minutes. After they had listed all that the other side had got up to, they began to get more personal.

'Why don't you come over here and say that?' yelled the fishermen. 'Don't we want to get our little feet wet?'

'Come and get a taste of our concrete clogs,'

replied the farmers, slapping the concrete boots they wore so as not to blow away in strong winds.

I noticed that none of them got any closer, when they shouted all this. In fact they were careful not to move too much in case the other side came at them when they weren't prepared.

'You didn't see us do it, did you, though?' asked a farmer, red in the face from all the shouting.

'I suppose it was one of our lot, then, was it?' asked a fisherman, getting red in the face himself. 'Come to that, I suppose it's true the other way round, isn't it?'

'How do you mean?' asked the same farmer, suspiciously.

'No one saw anyone doing the things that happened to us!' replied the fisherman.

The farmer went very thoughtful about this, as did everyone on both sides who was anywhere near and might have heard. (About half of them, I think.)

There was a lot of muttering on both sides, and a lot of heads were put together. Plover spotted this and he and the Chief Farmer put *their* heads together. Not a pretty sight.

Then the Chief Farmer moved to the front of the line. He motioned to the farmers to be quiet, which they didn't. He then ignored them, and shouted over to the fishermen: 'I would like to believe you. If you can PROVE what you say, we'll agree to call off the fighting.'

This was a GOOD THING, I thought, until I noticed that Plover had a very wicked smile on his face. Then an EVIL THOUGHT struck me. 'Ow,' I said, rubbing the place where it hit me. The EVIL THOUGHT struck me again. This time I was too brave to say 'Ow'. I rubbed the bruises and carried on thinking. No one could possibly *prove* anything because no one had *seen* anything. And Plover knew it.

There was a slight rumbling noise at the other end of the cliff, but no one took any notice. Except me, and I couldn't see what it was.

The two sides went back to shouting things at each other, and called each other most of the things I call people when I call them names, together with a few new ones that I didn't know. Maybe it might be more fun being grown-up than I thought. This time I could tell that things were going to get really nasty. But what could I do? There's just one of me, and lots of them.

The shouting then moved up to the far end, as the farmers near me had gone all thoughtful again. There was a lot of noise and the word 'WHALE' kept being repeated.

As it looked like the fighting was going to start for real this time, I thought about escaping up the cliff again to try and find the bulldozer. It sounds silly, but I really wanted to be where the bulldozer was.

I picked up the fork, and turned round ready to run. But I hadn't gone three steps when the shouting moved back down to my end of the beach. 'WHERE IS THE WHALE? WHERE IS THE WHALE?'

I later found out that the farmers were all shouting this at Plover, because they knew he'd stolen it and then let it escape. And the fishermen were all shouting it because somebody had spread the word round that the whale had escaped. And they all wanted to know where it was. I thought of all the things that could happen. There weren't any more pitchforks or onions for fighting with. But the farmers still had their concrete clogs, and the fishermen still had their nets. I didn't have a PLAN, I didn't even have the bulldozer. Where was Uncle Joe? Where was the King of the Fishermen? WHERE WAS THE WHALE?

I began to think worse thoughts. What would the world be like without fish-and-chips? I'd walk down the street and into the shop on the corner and say: 'A portion of … um … er … er … well … nothing.' And Big John (who owns the chip-shop on the corner) would look at me with sad eyes from behind a counter full of nothing and give me an empty bag. I couldn't face the thought any more. But what was I to do?

The whale itself provided the answer to all this. It arrived at the far end of the beach bringing a huge wave, even bigger than the last big wave, sweeping along the shore. The farmers were all washed off their feet, and the fishermen soon had them surrounded and tied up in nets. Then they made a big

pile of all the farmers' concrete clogs on one side, out of the way. Just in case anyone should start having ideas about doing something with them. Things looked BAD. The battle wasn't supposed to end this way. Suppose the fishermen decided to.... I sat down and thought of all the things that the fishermen might do to punish the farmers for starting it all. (But the farmers hadn't started it all. It was Plover.) There were a lot of dreadful things, and if they did even half of them, there would be no farmers left and the world would have to end because of there being no fish-and-chips. If there's no one to grow potatoes, there will be no potatoes to make chips with, will there? I put my head in my hands and sat there worrying and picking my lip.

There seemed to be no way of sorting this mess out. I stood up and walked up the cliff a little way.

Suddenly, from behind a hump in the ground an old black car appeared. And in the old black car was Traplot the poacher, with a big grin on his face. He got out and walked over to me.

'Aha, there you are,' he said. 'I have a secret to tell 'ee, young man.' And he tugged at his ear. 'Just you come here, mmm, and take a look at this.'

I went over carefully, in case this was one of his little jokes that might turn into a trap.

'Now,' he said and pointed down at the beach. I watched as the fishermen made a big circle round the farmers, and took hold of the ends of the nets. They then tried to roll the nets up, to wash the farmers out to sea. But as they did, they seemed to get caught up in the net themselves. I couldn't believe my eyes! Within a few seconds, the farmers and the fishermen were both tied up in the same nets. And they were so well tied up that they

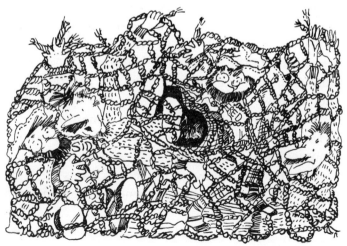

couldn't do anything to each other.

Traplot looked at me. 'Aha,' he said, and tugged at his ear. 'That shows you what happens if you try to be too tricky. You get caught up in your own nets. I made those nets. I made them in a special way to stop people being too tricksy with them. Now we shall have to go down and sort things out properly. Come with me.'

I got into his old black car. He got in too and started the engine. The car didn't go very fast, so we had plenty of time to talk in.

'I looked for you after you went,' he said.

'Why?' I asked. I don't mess about, you know.

'Because I was so stuck. But in the end I was too tricksy for the car. It couldn't keep me trapped for long. Though 'tis sometimes useful to have someone standing by. That way the car will know 'tis outnumbered.'

'What are we going to do with everyone?' I asked. After all things still weren't properly sorted out. Where was Plover? Where were Figgis, Bloodeye and Twistel? Where was the whale? As these questions went through my head, Traplot pointed out of the window.

'Just you look over there, young man.'

I don't usually go along with people who call me 'young man', but I decided I would this time. I looked, and just below us on the beach was the King of the Fishermen! He had turned up again, in a

green frogman's suit, with his crown tied on with red string. And there was the whale! It was stuck in the shallow water, but didn't seem to be too bothered. The King was saying nice things, and scratching the whale every so often, like you might with a cat. Every so often he looked round to make sure no one was watching him. Traplot stopped the car so we could hear what he was saying. He wasn't saying anything when we arrived above him, and said even less after we arrived. At last he looked at the whale and said, rather loudly, 'I'm glad you came back.'

Traplot started up the car and we drove on down to find the bulldozer and Uncle Joe.

The bulldozer wasn't hard to find, as it had just started to go down a bit of the cliff that wasn't too steep. This made it easier for us to go down after them.

I could see Van chewing his knuckles and the fortune-teller chewing her nails. And I was really busy looking for Uncle Joe in all the crowd of tied-up people. Where was he?

When we did at last get to the bottom of the cliff, Van took the bulldozer off to clear away the rocks. That's what he said he was going to do, anyway. 'I'm taking this bulldozer off to clear away the rocks', he said.

Traplot and I got out of the car. He went off to untie everyone, and I started looking for My Uncle. I found him in a corner, talking in a low voice to a circle of cross-legged men, and wiping his hands on an oily rag. He was also smoking a pipe rather quickly. This usually meant that he was angry about something. And sure enough, he was.

'If one of you has let Plover get away . . .' he was just saying as I walked up. 'If one of you has let *anyone* get away . . .' he said, snapping his pipe in two and lighting another one.

The circle of men didn't wait for him to finish the sentence, but jumped to their feet and scampered off in all directions.

Uncle Joe didn't notice me at first, but went over to a large green coil of rope. I thought I'd seen the coil somewhere before, but I wasn't sure. I looked round to see if I could recognize anyone else, but I couldn't. Everyone looked rather cold and miserable.

I turned back to Uncle Joe. He was just giving the rope a huge great big kick. The coil of rope snorted, turned over, and went back to sleep. I went over and tickled the rope with the toasting-fork. That certainly woke it up. It was the python, and it gave me another verse of its poem as a punishment:

'Spare a thought for men like these,
Making doughnuts on bended knees,
They bake them and fry them and stuff them with jam,
To sell them pell-mell like so much flim-flam.'

I said I was sorry and the python agreed to save the next verse for another time.

I went up to Uncle Joe and gave him a *big hug* and he looked rather surprised. So surprised that he dropped his oily rag. The sun came out from behind a cloud, but thought better of it and disappeared again. Uncle Joe squinted at me to make sure it was me, then grinned a lot. I didn't know he could do that sort of thing with his face.

'When we do find Plover and all his evil friends, we'll make them tell everyone what they were up to. That should stop the fighting for ever.'

There was a lot of crashing and rumbling from the other end of the beach as he said this. I turned, and saw that Van and the fortune-teller had piled the rocks up to make a sort of platform.

'How did you know things were going to turn out like this?' I asked. 'And how did you know that everyone would get caught up in the nets?'

Uncle Joe looked mysterious, and lit his pipe again. 'I have ways of finding things out,' he said. 'How do you think I found out about Boris the lion? I just have ways of finding things out.'

This was all too much for me and I just stood there gaping. How could I have thought that Uncle Joe was boring? Too much was happening all too quickly. I had to sit down and think about it.

After a long think, I still hadn't got any further with it, so I stood up again.

By this time, Uncle Joe had gone off somewhere. I looked to see if anyone was untied yet, but they weren't. Perhaps Traplot had tied himself up in his own knots.

The King of the Fishermen had now stopped scratching the whale's head, and was tracing the shape of a chessboard in the sand with his big toe. The whale looked a bit grumpy at being out of the water, and was trying to roll back in. Then it began to hiccup. It hiccupped three times, and on the third time it sneezed as well. And when it sneezed, five figures ran out of its mouth, covered in seaweed. It was Plover, Bloodeye, Figgis, Twistel and the Chief Farmer, and they were all soaked and very fishy.

Just to show that there were no hard feelings, I took out the toasting-fork and dried them out. I turned it down low to make sure they didn't get burned. Even so, Figgis did look a bit smoky round the edges. Well it was his fault for being so big and

fat, wasn't it?

As soon as this evil lot appeared from out of the whale's mouth, the python nipped over and wrapped them up in five very snug coils. It then dragged them up onto the platform that Van and the fortune-teller had just made.

'Oh,' they both said, 'we were just about to clear all this away and . . . .' They stopped when they saw the size of the python.

When the python had lined all five up, he made a loud noise to make sure everyone was watching. He needn't have, because all the farmers and fishermen were watching everything that Van did. There wasn't anything else to watch, and they were still all tied up. I noticed Traplot, right in the middle of it all, tying and untying all kinds of strange knots.

All five villains looked very seasick, and in no mood to argue. 'Tell them it was all your fault,' hissed the python, squeezing Plover till he squeaked.

'No, it wasn't my fault,' he said, trying hard to breathe. 'It was ooooooOOOOoo.' Here the python squeezed him again. Plover didn't seem to be beaten yet.

'I tricked you all,' he said.

There was a lot of booing at this. Plover snarled and showed his teeth. The python squeezed again.

'I wanted to steal all the . . . oooo potatoes and the fish AND EAT THEM MYSELF.'

There was a long silence.

'How would you like being so thin?' Plover cried. Everyone else here is a nice shape. If they're not nice and fat, they're thin and tall. I'm short and skinny. I always wanted to be REALLY REALLY FAT one day, but you rotten lot wouldn't let me. That's why I wanted to keep you all fighting, so that I could sneak off and. . . .' At this point he fainted and had to be fanned with someone's hat.

'But I thought I was going to get it all,' said Figgis, puzzled. 'I thought that I was going to eat it all, Plover? Plover? Speak to me, Plover . . .'

Everyone laughed at this, and Figgis saw that he was beaten. Bloodeye and Twistel were too busy sneezing to say much but they muttered about how sorry they were and promised to be good in future.

Everyone cheered at this, and the snake let the three of them go. They slunk away off the rock platform, and began untying everyone else. There was more cheering.

Plover and the Chief Farmer still had to be dealt with. Uncle Joe got up on the platform and had a few words in the Chief Farmer's ears.

The Chief Farmer hung his head and looked a bit sheepish. 'I should never have trusted Plover,' he said. 'I don't think I've been a very good chief. Someone else had better do it.' He stopped for a moment and sneezed several times, and then sat down.

There was a lot of talk among the farmers about who should be the new chief, but at that moment, Van happened to walk on to the platform. As he was the only one of the farmers not tied up, the Chief took hold of his hand. 'What about him?' he shouted to the rest of the farmers.

'Who?' shouted most of the farmers, as they weren't all facing the same way and couldn't see him. 'Van,' said the Chief Farmer.

There was a short pause while they thought about it.

'Why?' said a voice that I'd heard before. I looked to see who it was. It was the man in the black hat who had been so angry when he found out that the pitchforks had all been burned. He certainly wasn't messing about with his questions this time.

'Why not?' said everybody else.

'No special reason,' said the man in the black hat. 'Let's have Van for our chief, and stop all this fighting. Three cheers for Van!' Everybody cheered again. So Van was made chief on the spot. He blushed a lot and tried to smile quietly to himself, and then went off to talk to the rest of the farmers. Before he left the platform he turned and yelled, 'NO MORE FIGHTING,' to the crowd. Everyone took up the cry and began hugging each other. The Chief Farmer was released and went over to the King of the Fishermen. They both sat down and began to play chess in the sand. I stepped up on to the platform to see what would happen to Plover.

The snake seemed to have brought him round and was trying out another verse of his poem.

> *'Don't think that one thought will help these bakers,*
> *Escape the coils of wily fakers,*
> *Who lurk by every murky pool,*
> *Upon the backs of dancing bears.*
> *Who cares?'*

Plover sat up and tried to get away from the poem, but the snake seemed to want to make him listen to the whole thing. When the snake had finished,

Uncle Joe and Van appeared and gave him another SHARP TALKING TO about behaving himself. And Van told him that he'd have to work very hard on his farm if he wanted to stay here. Otherwise he'd have to go and work for Traplot and build traps.

Plover finally chose to go off with Traplot, who'd managed to get everyone out of the nets, and get the nets all stowed away back in the boats. They disappeared off in Traplot's old black car, which coughed a lot. Before they had gone twenty yards, they'd started arguing. But I was sure that Traplot was just as tricky as Plover. And he was fatter. Maybe Plover would change in time if he ate more.

Van said goodbye, as he was going to tidy things up a bit in the Chief Farmer's cave. The fortune-teller went with him, because she wanted to take the bulldozer engine apart. She gave me the crystal ball because she didn't want it, and the snake grabbed it from me, quick as a flash. Just as well because I didn't want it.

The farmers and fishermen were now getting very friendly with each other and there was a lot of backslapping and stamping of feet and puffing of pipes. They waved goodbye to the three of us as we went sadly down the beach to see the King and the ex-Chief.

The whale had got back into deeper water by now, and was swimming up and down and singing in a very eerie high-pitched voice. The King and the ex-Chief had agreed on a draw in their game of chess and were looking at the whale. The King of the Fishermen had a faraway look in his eye.

'I must be going as well,' he said to us when we told him that we had to go. 'But my friend the old Chief of the Farmers is going to come and live with me and play chess. Perhaps the python would like to come as well? I like that poem that begins 'Bearded Fishlock sits in his den....'

The snake said he would and we said a very long goodbye to the three of them.

'Before you go,' said the King, 'you will try to be kind to whales, won't you? The python was telling me that some people go hunting them with harpoons. I can't think why. Goodbye.'

And they were gone, on the back of the whale. The fishermen all got into their boats and followed him out to sea, waving and cheering as they did so.

We watched them go out of sight, sadly, because we wanted to stay a bit longer. The only people left besides us were Figgis, Bloodeye and Twistel, who were tidying things up on the beach.

They were done at last and hurried off after the farmers, looking round to make sure that the python wasn't after them. I'm still not sure about that python. He was getting above himself. But still, we couldn't stay to sort him out. We had to leave everyone to get on with things. 'Will the toasting-fork get us home?' I asked Uncle Joe.

He scratched in the sand with it, and said nothing. I tried again.

'Have you got another balloon?'

He said even more nothing than before. With my tiny fists, I took the toasting-fork from him. He said nothing again.

I wasn't quite sure how to get home, but I had an idea. If the toasting-fork could go as fast as the

balloon, we might be home in time to eat a little something. All I had to do was tie Uncle Joe and me to it and point the fork in the right direction. Perhaps the fork knew anyway.

I took Uncle Joe's hand and wrapped it round the fork. Then I took hold of the fork, whispered, 'Let's go home,' and pressed what I thought was the right sort of button. There was a BANG and most of Uncle Joe's eyebrows were blown off, but the fork started to move. It took us up over the hill, too fast to wave goodbye to everyone again, then it went faster and I had to shut my eyes.

And before long we were back in the living-room as if nothing had happened. Well, not quite nothing.

'I've got wet feet,' I said.

'Me, too,' said Uncle Joe, smoking no pipe at all.

And I still had to do the washing-up.

What an adventure. But honestly, I did it all, really, didn't I? Apart from a few accidents. My Uncle had nothing to do with it. That's my story and I'm sticking to it.